DOMESTIC WIRETAPPING
IN THE WAR ON TERROR

Domestic Wiretapping in the War on Terror

A Briefing Before
The United States Commission on Civil Rights
Held in Washington, DC

Briefing Report

Table of Contents

Briefing and Subsequent Events

On March 9, 2007, a panel of three experts attended a briefing on domestic wiretapping in the war on terror at the U.S. Commission on Civil Rights. Gregory T. Nojeim, Assistant Director and Chief Legislative Counsel of the American Civil Liberties Union, Washington Legislative Office; Dr. John Eastman, Professor at Chapman University School of Law and Director of the Claremont Institute Center for Constitutional Jurisprudence; and Kareem W. Shora, National Executive Director of the American-Arab Anti Discrimination Committee presented their insights on the constitutional implications of wiretapping in the war on terror, the role of the President and Congress in national security policy-making and program authorization, and the impact of surveillance programs on Arab Americans and other groups. The briefing was held in Room 540 at 624 Ninth Street, Northwest, Washington, DC.

The briefing was originally scheduled in response to Bush administration policies generally described as the Terrorist Surveillance Program (TSP). In general terms, the dispute focused on the fact that, in 2002, President George W. Bush secretly authorized the National Security Agency to conduct warrantless phone-taps of domestic targets reasonably believed to be in communication with a member or agent of al Qaeda, or an affiliated terrorist organization. Supporters of this program argued that the President has the constitutional and statutory authority to conduct such warrantless phone taps. Critics, on the other hand, argued that the program violated the Foreign Intelligence Surveillance Act (FISA), which permits warrantless taps of 72 hours, but otherwise requires an order from a Foreign Intelligence Surveillance Court. Critics also argued that these taps did not comport with the Fourth Amendment prohibition against unreasonable searches and seizures.

Shortly before the briefing, however, the Bush administration indicated that it would not reauthorize the TSP when the current authorization expired. Specifically, on January 17, 2007, U.S. Attorney General Alberto Gonzalez sent a letter to senators Patrick Leahy and Arlen Specter of the Senate Judiciary Committee providing, in part:

> [O]n January 10, 2007, a Judge of the Foreign Intelligence Surveillance Court had issued orders authorizing the Government to target for collection international communications into or out of the United States where there is probable cause to believe that one of the communicants is a member or agent of al Qaeda or an associated terrorist organization. As a result of these orders, any electronic surveillance that was occurring as part of the Terrorist Surveillance Program will now be conducted subject to the approval of the Foreign Intelligence Surveillance Court.

Subsequent to the briefing, Congress enacted the Protect America Act (*see* 50 U.S.C. § 8108, *et seq.* (2007)). This legislation allowed the government to intercept and record electronic communications, without a warrant, when the communications involved people reasonably believed to be outside the United States. The law was signed on August 5, 2007, and lapsed on February 6, 2008.

Thereafter, Congress enacted the Foreign Intelligence Surveillance Act (FISA) Amendments Act of 2008 (*see* 50 U.S.C. § 1881c (2008)). Among other things, the act requires individual

FISA court orders, based on probable cause, for the surveillance or monitoring of American citizens regardless of whether they are within or outside the United States. The act also provides standards and procedures for liability protection for electronic communication service providers who assist the government following the attacks of September 11, 2001.

A transcript of the briefing is available on the Commission's Web site (www.usccr.gov), and by request from the Publications Office, U.S. Commission on Civil Rights, 624 Ninth Street, NW, Suite 600, Washington, DC 20425, (202) 376-8128, TTY (202) 376-8116, or via e-mail at publications@usccr.gov.

Summary of Proceedings

Gregory T. Nojeim

Mr. Nojeim began by outlining the history of presidential warrantless wiretapping and the background events that had led up to the passing of the Foreign Intelligence Surveillance Act (FISA). He argued that the Bush administration's warrantless wiretapping program conducted from 2002 to 2007, violated the Fourth Amendment[1] right to be secure against unreasonable searches and seizures. Mr. Nojeim asserted that, although the Bush administration claimed that these wiretaps were authorized according to the Authorization for the Use of Military Force Act (AUMF),[2] enacted in September 2001, there is no evidence that Congress intended the president to be able to override the provisions of FISA,[3] which require obtaining a warrant for any surveillance involving U.S. persons. Mr. Nojeim noted that Congress had enacted over 25 changes to FISA within 40 days of passing AUMF,[4] as well as in subsequent years, and yet had not struck the requirement that surveillance be conducted with judicial approval. He argued that Congress' failure to make such a change indicated a continuing legal obligation by the Bush administration to follow FISA regardless of the passage of AUMF.[5]

Mr. Nojeim discussed a Michigan lawsuit filed by the American Civil Liberties Union (ACLU) against the Bush administration's warrantless wiretapping program, in which a district court ruled that the program violated the First Amendment, Fourth Amendment, and FISA.[6] He quoted the judge in the case as saying that the framers of the Constitution never meant for the president to have such unfettered control, and that the Bush administration's actions were in violation of the Bill of Rights. Mr. Nojeim then noted that this case is currently on appeal.[7]

---

[1] U.S. CONST. amend. IV.

[2] Pub. L. No. 107-40, 115 Stat. 224 (2001).

[3] 50 U.S.C. § 1805 (2000).

[4] *See* USA PATRIOT Act, Pub. L. No. 107-56, 115 Stat. 272 (2001).

[5] Gregory T. Nojeim, Testimony before the U.S. Commission on Civil Rights, briefing, Washington, DC, Mar. 9, 2007, transcript, pp. 6–9 (hereafter cited as Nojeim Testimony, Briefing Transcript).

[6] In *ACLU v. National Sec. Agency*, the District Court held that "the Fourth Amendment…requires reasonableness in all searches. It also requires prior warrants for any reasonable search, based upon prior-existing probable cause, as well as particularity as to persons, places, and things, and the interposition of a neutral magistrate between Executive branch enforcement officers and citizens. In enacting FISA, Congress made numerous concessions to stated executive needs…[t]he wiretapping program here in litigation has undisputedly been continued for at least five years, it has undisputedly been implemented without regard to FISA and of course the more stringent standards of Title III, and obviously in violation of the Fourth Amendment." *ACLU v. National Sec. Agency*, 438 F. Supp. 2d 754, 775 (E.D. Mich., 2006), *vacated*, 493 F.3d 644 (6th Cir. 2007).

[7] Nojeim Testimony, Briefing Transcript, pp. 9–10. Subsequent to the Commission's briefing, the 6th Circuit Court of Appeals vacated the decision of *ACLU v. National Sec. Agency*, 438 F. Supp. 2d 754, 775 (E.D. Mich., 2006). The court held that the plaintiff lacked standing to sue on their First and Fourth Amendment claims, writing that "[i]n crafting their declaratory judgment action, the plaintiffs have attempted (unsuccessfully) to navigate the obstacles to stating a justiciable claim. By refraining from communications (i.e., the potentially

Mr. Nojeim said that the Bush administration announced that it had abandoned its warrantless wiretapping program in January of 2007 in favor of a program that is subject to FISA court approval. He noted, however, that the administration still claimed the inherent authority for the president to engage in warrantless eavesdropping. He stated that at no point had the president agreed to abandon warrantless surveillance.[8]

Mr. Nojeim then listed questions that he believed remained unanswered about the government's process to secure approval by the FISA court: Why did it take two years to get the approval of just one of 15 FISA court judges? Which other judges were approached to approve the program? What kind of innovative arrangement was used to obtain the approval? To what extent did the government release information to the public to help clarify whether an order met the requirements of FISA?[9]

Mr. Nojeim discussed the difficulty in determining whether the government was getting individualized warrants based on individualized suspicion, or whether it was obtaining "program warrants" that do not require individualized suspicion of wrongdoing. He noted that the Bush administration refused to answer this question despite Congressional inquiry into the matter, and said he believed that both FISA and the Fourth Amendment require that warrants be obtained based on individual suspicion.[10]

Elaborating on some of the aforementioned issues, Mr. Nojeim then identified the concerns he had with "program warrants." He stated that the Fourth Amendment prohibited program warrants and that their misuse was one of the reasons that Americans fought the Revolutionary War. He differentiated between individualized warrants, which involve investigative intrusion on identified wrongdoers, and program warrants, which make it more likely that federal agents will eavesdrop on conversations that do not involve anyone who is legitimately targeted for surveillance. Mr. Nojeim emphasized that the use of program warrants raises the possibility of unfocused intrusion upon many people who have done nothing wrong and who are not agents of foreign powers.[11]

---

harmful conduct), the plaintiffs have negated any possibility that the NSA will ever actually intercept their communications and thereby avoided the anticipated harm-this is typical of declaratory judgment and perfectly permissible. But, by proposing only injuries that *result* from this refusal to engage in communications (e.g., the inability to conduct their professions without added burden and expense), they attempt to supplant an insufficient, speculative injury with an injury that appears sufficiently imminent and concrete, but is only incidental to the alleged wrong (i.e., the NSA's conduct)—this is atypical and…impermissible." *ACLU v. National Sec. Agency*, 493 F.3d 644, 656-57 (6th Cir. 2007) (citation omitted). *cert. denied*, 128 S. Ct. 1334 (2008). The court also denied the plaintiff's claim that the Bush Administration's warrantless wiretapping program violated FISA, holding that "[t]he plaintiffs have not shown, and cannot show, that the NSA's surveillance activities include the sort of conduct that would satisfy FISA's definition of 'electronic surveillance,' and the present record does not demonstrate that the NSA's conduct falls within FISA's definitions." *Id.* at 682.

[8] Nojeim Testimony, Briefing Transcript, p. 10.

[9] Ibid., p. 10.

[10] Ibid., pp. 10–11.

[11] Ibid., p. 11.

Next, Mr. Nojeim asserted that, regardless of whether the new surveillance program complies with FISA, it does not excuse those responsible for five years of illegal surveillance. He again questioned why the Bush administration did not comply with FISA in the first place.[12]

Turning to the beliefs of the ACLU, Mr. Nojeim said that the ACLU contends that privacy need not be sacrificed for security. He argued that, for almost 30 years, FISA has been successfully protecting both of these important values, and that warrantless wiretapping outside of FISA regulations was a violation of a criminal statute. He urged the Commission to insist that the government disclose the steps it is taking so as to minimize the damage that the program has done to Americans' privacy and to call for accountability for illegal conduct.[13]

In concluding, Mr. Nojeim stressed that the government needs to be called to account for five years of illegal warrantless wiretapping, and that the lack of disclosure about this new program is troubling. He recommended that the Commission conduct formal hearings on this issue and asked that it request Congress to do the same.[14]

John C. Eastman

Dr. Eastman began by questioning the Commission's authority to look into alleged violations of civil liberties that were of a generalized nature, rather than a specific racial, ethnic, or religious nature as mandated by its statutory authority. He said that he assumed that there would be a discussion as to whether there is a problem of jurisdiction, as he had not seen any evidence that the Commission was authorized to look into the matter of wireless surveillance. He stated that, for the moment, he would assume that there was a legitimate, legal authority behind the Commission's decision to hold a hearing on wiretapping.[15]

Dr. Eastman began his substantive discussion by saying that, the district judge in Michigan notwithstanding, the president does have the authority to operate warrantless wiretaps.[16] He stated that when the *New York Times* broke the warrantless wiretap story in December of 2005,[17] there were two competing papers that had been published: one by the Congressional Research Service,[18] and another by the Department of Justice.[19] Dr. Eastman expressed his belief that the Department of Justice's position was much better grounded in history, text, and legal services, and that, in his view, the White House had been trying to comply with

[12] Ibid., pp. 11–12.

[13] Ibid., p. 12.

[14] Ibid., pp. 12–13.

[15] John C. Eastman, Testimony before the U.S. Commission on Civil Rights, briefing, Washington, DC, Mar. 9, 2007, transcript, pp. 14–15 (hereafter Eastman Testimony, Briefing Transcript).

[16] This history of this case is discussed in footnotes 6 and 7, *supra*.

[17] James Risen & Eric Lichtblau, "Bush Lets U.S. Spy on Callers Without Courts," *New York Times*, Dec. 16, 2005, p. A1.

[18] Elizabeth B. Bazan and Jennifer K. Elsea, Congressional Research Memorandum, "Presidential Authority to Conduct Warrantless Electronic Surveillance to Gather Foreign Intelligence Information" (Jan. 5, 2006).

[19] The paper by the Department of Justice is available at http:www.usdoj.gov/ag/readingroom/surveillance6.pdf.

every possible law and precedent while trying to protect the U.S. after the attacks of September 11, 2001.[20]

Dr. Eastman then identified what he believed to be two different lines of authority for the president's surveillance program. The first was the AUMF; Dr. Eastman acknowledged that although Mr. Nojeim and the ACLU disagreed, the U.S. Supreme Court had already addressed the scope of FISA in an analogous context and had rejected the ACLU's argument. The second source of authority Dr. Eastman relied upon was based on an analogy to the Anti-Detention Act.[21] He described the reasons the president had presented for claiming the authority to detain U.S. citizens and others, and how this authority was challenged as a violation of that act. Dr. Eastman noted that in *Hamdi v. Rumsfeld*,[22] the Supreme Court had considered the detention of enemy combatants to be an inherent part of the war power that had been authorized by the AUMF. In Dr. Eastman's opinion, the ability to conduct surveillance of enemy communications is so central to the war powers given to the president under the AUMF that it has to be viewed as authorizing the president to conduct this program, analogous to the detention situation in *Hamdi*.[23]

Dr. Eastman then discussed how the letters of his grandfather, a U.S. soldier serving abroad in World War I, were censored so as not to reveal any classified information. Dr. Eastman stressed that there were no warrants collected before the government engaged in the surveillance needed to preemptively censor those letters, and that the matter involved U.S. citizens and not enemy combatants. Dr. Eastman continued saying that, in times of war, we need to recognize that the reasonableness requirement of the Fourth Amendment is different than during peacetime, noting that the president has never before had to seek warrants to intercept enemy communications during war.[24]

Dr. Eastman then gave his opinion that the authorization for the use of force broadened existing statutory authority granted to the president relating to surveillance. Even if it does not, Dr. Eastman argued that the analysis in Justice Jackson's concurring opinion in the case of *Youngstown Sheet & Tube*,[25] describing three categories for analyzing separation of power

---

[20] Eastman Testimony, Briefing Transcript, pp. 15–16.

[21] 18 U.S.C. § 4001(a) (2009).

[22] *Hamdi v. Rumsfeld*, 542 U.S. 507, 518 (2004).

[23] Eastman Testimony, Briefing Transcript, p. 17.

[24] Ibid., p. 18.

[25] In *Youngstown Sheet & Tube Co. v. Sawyer*, 343 U.S. 579 (1952), a conflict arose when President Truman attempted to seize private steel processing facilities rather than see them close due to a strike during the Korean War. Truman's actions were directly opposed by Congress, which refused to pass emergency legislation to validate the seizure. In ruling that the President had exceeded his wartime authority, Justice Jackson's concurrence delineated three separate categories of executive action. In Category One, "the President acts pursuant to an express or implied authorization of Congress [and] his authority is at its maximum, for it includes all that he possesses in his own right plus all that Congress can delegate. 343 U.S. at 635–37 (1952) (citation omitted) (Jackson, J., concurring). In Category Two, "the President acts in absence of either a congressional grant or denial of authority [and] he can only rely upon his own independent powers, but there is a zone of twilight in which he and Congress may have concurrent authority, or in which its distribution is uncertain. Therefore, congressional inertia, indifference or quiescence may sometimes, at least as a practical matter, enable, if not invite, measures on independent presidential responsibility. In this area, any actual test of power is

issues when presidential and congressional powers intersect, gives the president the Constitutional authority to run a warrantless wiretap program. Dr. Eastman said that he believes the Bush administration's warrantless wiretap program fits into Category One of Justice Jackson's analysis, wherein a president acts with authorization from a statute of Congress, and the president's power is at its apex, because Congress authorized the use of force in the AUMF. Dr. Eastman noted that, even when a president's actions fall into Category Three (when the president acts contrary to explicit statutory authority of Congress), the president's power is not non-existent, but merely at its lowest ebb. He then pointed out that the current situation presented a stronger case for presidential authority than was the case in *Youngstown Sheet & Tube*, in that the present conflict involved attacks within the United States which resulted in an explicit authorization of force by Congress.[26]

Dr. Eastman stated that the attacks of September 11th made it vividly clear that American soil is part of the battlefield of the war on terror. He said that the most important front in that war is not abroad, but at home. For the intelligence-gathering community to be able to preemptively prevent enemy attack, it must discover where and when those attacks will occur. He expressed his opinion that information is the most critical tool our military has and that to say that the president does not have inherent authority to obtain such information is to ignore the founders' design of presidential power.[27]

Dr. Eastman also noted that in FISA and its precursors, Congress explicitly recognized that the president has certain inherent authority in matters of war. He mentioned testimony from Griffin Bell, President Carter's attorney general, wherein Bell said that FISA does not diminish the president's Constitutional authority. He also noted that in 1994, President Clinton's deputy attorney general, Jamie Gorelick, said that the Department of Justice believed, and case law supported, the contention that the president has inherent authority to conduct warrantless physical searches for foreign intelligence purposes.[28]

Turning to case law, Dr. Eastman noted that in *In Re: Sealed Case*,[29] the FISA Court of Appeals said in *dicta* that it assumed that the president has the inherent authority to conduct

---

likely to depend on the imperatives of events and contemporary imponderables rather than on abstract theories of law." *Id.* at 637 (citation omitted). Finally, Category Three is when "the President takes measures incompatible with the expressed or implied will of Congress [and] his power is at its lowest ebb, for then he can rely only upon his own constitutional powers minus any constitutional powers of Congress over the matter. Courts can sustain exclusive Presidential control in such a case only by disabling the Congress from acting upon the subject. Presidential claim to a power at once so conclusive and preclusive must be scrutinized with caution, for what is at stake is the equilibrium established by our constitutional system." *Id.* at 637–38 (citation omitted).

[26] Eastman Testimony, Briefing Transcript, pp.18–20.

[27] Ibid., pp. 20–21.

[28] Ibid., pp. 21–22.

[29] In *In Re: Sealed Case*, 310 F.3d 717 (Foreign Int. Surv. Ct. Rev. 2002), the FISA Court of Review held that FISA is constitutional, that the minimization requirements of FISA are not grounds to limit the purpose of the FISA application, and that FISA may be used to collect evidence for criminal prosecution. They also stated that "all the other courts to have decided the issue [of warrantless wiretapping have] held that the President did have inherent authority to conduct warrantless searches to obtain foreign intelligence information…we take for granted that the President does have that authority and, assuming that is so, FISA could not encroach on the President's constitutional power." 310 F.3d 717 at 742.

warrantless wiretaps, and that to interpret FISA as limiting that authority would render FISA unconstitutional.[30]

Dr. Eastman concluded by saying that it was important for the Commission to begin its investigation into civil rights violations with the understanding that, during wartime, the president has the authority to monitor conversations wherein one party has been identified as an enemy or working with enemies of the United States. He stated that the president has never before been required to produce a warrant for such actions, as they derive directly from Article 2 of the Constitution, and that we have never second guessed the president's war authority or forced the president to ask permission of the courts before he takes action to defend America.[31]

Kareem W. Shora

Mr. Shora began by briefly outlining the history of the American-Arab Anti Discrimination Committee (ADC). He described the action taken by the U.S. government in the wake of 9/11 as being unfortunate, ineffective, and largely cosmetic. He claimed further that, in his view, it left a bitter taste within the Arab, Muslim, and South Asian American communities, and was a mark of shame on American society.[32]

Mr. Shora noted that, in fairness, the government had taken some constructive, proactive steps at conducting regular dialogue with the ADC as well as Arab, Muslim, and South Asian American communities. He stated that this dialogue addressed some serious rights violations, and that the Arab American community wanted to publicly acknowledge their gratitude for such discourse.[33]

Turning to the role of Arab Americans, Mr. Shora said that since 9/11, the Arab community has recognized the special role that it has with law enforcement and other government agencies. He stated that ADC and others knew of multiple examples of Arabs standing shoulder to shoulder with law enforcement agencies. Specifically, he mentioned the diversity and law enforcement outreach program that the ADC began in 2002. Mr. Shora noted that this program has trained approximately 8,000 law enforcement officials in cultural competency by teaching them to effectively and expertly differentiate between actual threats and behavior based on cultural norms and mores in Arab and Islamic culture. Additionally, Mr. Shora stated that he and his agency have provided law enforcement across the country with local partners available to coordinate legitimate law enforcement efforts on a case-by-case basis.[34]

Mr. Shora then addressed the government's unsolved challenges involving the Arab community, specifically, problems with the substance and perception of the warrantless

---

[30] Eastman Testimony, Briefing Transcript, p. 22.

[31] Ibid., pp. 22–23.

[32] Kareem W. Shora, Testimony before the U.S. Commission on Civil Rights, briefing, Washington, DC, Mar. 9, 2007, Transcript, pp. 24–25 (hereafter Shora Testimony, Briefing Transcript).

[33] Shora Testimony, Briefing Transcript, p. 25.

[34] Ibid., pp. 25–26.

domestic spying program. He believed that many of the counter-terrorism programs initiated by the Bush administration in 2001 and 2002 directly targeted Arab communities based solely on national origin. As examples of targeted efforts against Arabs, he cited programs such as the National Security Entry-Exit Registration System, the Federal Bureau of Investigation's (FBI) "voluntary interview initiatives," and the challenges associated with the multiple watch and no-fly lists. He asserted that, in defending these programs, the Bush administration had not identified even a single terrorist charged as a result of the programs. The only effect of these programs, he claimed, was to place an unwarranted spotlight on Arab communities.[35]

Turning to the domestic spying program, Mr. Shora claimed that, in 2003, President Bush ordered the National Security Agency (NSA), to illegally spy on American citizens by monitoring their electronic communications. He noted that later information and congressional testimony had made it clear that communication between the U.S. and the Middle East was the target of this initiative. He contended that, while national security should be at the forefront of government efforts, those efforts must be efficient, effective, and not self-defeating gestures that cost billions of dollars and force our intelligence agencies into a logjam of unprocessed data.[36]

Mr. Shora claimed that President Bush's authorization of the warrantless wiretap program violated the law and trampled on Americans' fundamental liberties and created apprehension in the Arab American community and the Middle East. Mr. Shora said that, although President Bush launched a public diplomacy campaign to "win the hearts and minds" of the people in the Middle East, the warrantless wiretap program had killed any chance of actually winning over anyone. American Arabs and Muslims, he said, are now afraid that if they communicate with their families abroad by phone, any conversation held in Arabic or another foreign language will be mistranslated and misunderstood by the NSA.[37]

Mr. Shora stated that it was shameful to see President Bush publicly and repeatedly defend the program, and that American citizens now assume that their conversations with relatives abroad are being monitored by government agencies with few resources and qualified professionals able to process the recorded information. He said that the American people need to ask themselves how they can promote democracy in the Middle East while the president routinely tramples upon it at home.[38]

Mr. Shora then said that the wiretapping program must be taken in context with other Bush administration War on Terror actions. He discussed the FBI's voluntary interview initiatives, demonstrating, in his view, that the FBI was abusing individual constitutional liberties in its assessment process. Mr. Shora noted that examples collected by the ADC have indicated that FBI and other law enforcement agents engaging in these interviews violate their parameters and engage in "patriotism tests" of Arab individuals. He alleged that questions about topics

---

[35] Ibid., pp. 26–27.

[36] Ibid., p. 27.

[37] Ibid., pp. 27–28.

[38] Ibid., pp. 28–29.

such as individual religious practices, and political views about the war in Iraq and the Palestinian-Israeli conflict, continue to be asked. Mr. Shora stated that these examples, although rare, have increased the negative perception the Arab and Muslim communities hold of the U.S. Government, FBI, and law enforcement in general, and have caused many to question whether there is a link between the FBI's domestic investigative efforts and the warrantless spying program.[39]

Mr. Shora then said that the U.S. government has yet to effectively address the misidentification of individuals whose names might be similar to those listed on a government watch or no-fly list. He relayed anecdotal evidence suggesting that Arab, Muslim, and South Asian Americans are more likely to be flagged by the Department of Homeland Security authorities when flying domestically or when returning from abroad. Mr. Shora noted that this included visitors, immigrants, and U.S. citizens equally. Although the Bush administration claimed not to use racial, ethnic, or religious profiling, in his view the watch and no-fly lists have instilled tremendous mistrust and a perception of ethnic and racial profiling in Arab and Muslim communities in the U.S.[40]

Mr. Shora continued by noting that, although the secret nature of the warrantless spying program precluded him from providing specific examples of the negative effects it has had on Arab communities, he did have anecdotal evidence to that effect. He described a 2004 incident that the ADC documented wherein an Arab American citizen, whom Mr. Shora referred to as Dr. Z, received a phone call from an FBI Special Agent. The agent courteously requested to speak to Dr. Z about telephone calls made between Dr. Z's home phone number and a country in the Middle East. Dr. Z then contacted the ADC to provide an attorney to monitor the meeting. The attorney said that, although courteous and professional, the FBI agent questioned Dr. Z for making regular phone calls to a specific city in the Arab world over a two-month period. When Dr. Z explained that he was calling his sick mother-in-law and his wife, who was visiting her, the FBI agent produced a copy of call logs made between Dr. Z's home and a specific area in the Arab city. When the ADC attorney asked if the FBI was monitoring Dr. Z's home and if they had a warrant to do so, the FBI stated allegedly that they were not, and that if they were, they would have produced a copy of the warrant to Dr. Z. According to Mr. Shora, the agent said that the call log was created by "intelligence sources" and not through any domestic FBI efforts, and that the agency was simply following up on a request to investigate. Mr. Shora concluded by saying that he would reserve his comments concerning the impact that the warrantless program has had on ADC public diplomacy efforts for the discussion.[41]

---

[39] Ibid., pp. 29–30.

[40] Ibid., pp. 30–31.

[41] Ibid., pp. 31–33.

Discussion

Commissioner Melendez asked Mr. Shora how widespread the perception is among the Arab American community that all Arab or Muslim Americans are having their calls tapped.[42] Mr. Shora responded that the perception is extremely prevalent, and has resulted in a reluctance to continue cooperative efforts with law enforcement agencies.[43]

Commissioner Braceras asked Mr. Shora what his role was in addressing the perception that those communities are wrongfully profiled; and, if he shared the belief that they are in fact being wrongfully profiled, on what evidence did he base that perception.[44] Mr. Shora replied that he relied on anecdotal evidence due to the secretive nature of the wireless surveillance.[45] Commissioner Braceras asked whether it was possible that Mr. Shora was fostering the perception of wrongful profiling.[46] Mr. Shora referred to his earlier anecdotal example, and indicated there were several other similar cases. He noted the difficulty in providing statistical data, as raw figures are available only to the Department of Justice.[47] Mr. Nojeim interceded and pointed to several examples of counter-terrorism programs the administration has launched which a focus on Arabs and Muslims. He suggested it would be unlikely for the program in question to not have focused on Arabs and Muslims given that the FBI and NSA have gone to such lengths to hire people who speak South Asian and Arabic languages.[48]

Commissioner Braceras agreed with Mr. Nojeim, but returned to her earlier question to Mr. Shora, regarding what obligation groups such as his have to dispel the perception that Arab American and Muslim American communities arc being wrongfully targeted, if such a perception is wrongly held.[49] Mr. Shora again replied that he does not believe the perception is based on myth, but on anecdotal examples directly reported to the ADC.[50] Commissioner Braceras countered that anecdotal examples are akin to urban legends, and have a tendency to take on a life of their own. She asked Mr. Shora for evidence of a widespread pattern of discriminatory conduct by law enforcement.[51]

Mr. Shora replied that he had already given three examples which he believed reflected systemic problems. He again referenced the National Security Entry/Exit Registration System (NSEERS), and the no-fly and watch-list programs.[52] Commissioner Braceras

---

[42] U.S. Commission on Civil Rights, briefing, Washington, DC, Mar. 9, 2007, transcript, p. 33, (hereafter Domestic Wiretapping, Briefing Transcript).

[43] Ibid., pp. 33–34.

[44] Ibid., p. 34.

[45] Ibid., p. 34.

[46] Ibid., p. 35.

[47] Ibid., p. 35.

[48] Ibid., pp. 35–36.

[49] Ibid., p. 36.

[50] Ibid., p. 37.

[51] Ibid., p. 37.

[52] Ibid., p. 37.

interjected and asked if Mr. Shora thought that the three cited examples reflected programs that incorrectly and erroneously targeted members of the Arab and Muslim community.[53] Mr. Shora responded by making reference to the testimony of Attorney General John Ashcroft before the Senate Judiciary Committee. Mr. Shora claimed that, in said testimony, the Attorney General was unable to point to a single charge of terrorism having been brought as a result of those programs, and could only point to several hundred deportation actions.[54]

Commissioner Braceras responded that there is a different evidentiary threshold between criminally charging individuals and deporting them. She asked Mr. Shora whether he believed individuals are wrongfully flagged on the basis of their race or ethnicity, or whether their race or ethnicity is incidental to other legitimate traits which raise red flags for the government.[55] Mr. Shora responded that he was unable to give a black and white answer because none existed, and that he could only provide the Commission with information that his organization received from around the country.[56]

Commissioner Taylor asked Mr. Nojeim if he could square the statements made by Mr. Shora based solely on anecdotal evidence and his assertion that the programs logically target ethnicities and races.[57] Mr. Nojeim cited the NSEERS program and pointed out that the administration has acknowledged targeting Arabs and Muslims. He also stated that, since the NSA and FBI recruits Arabic and South Asian speakers as opposed to Polish or Russian speakers, it is illogical to assume otherwise.[58]

Commissioner Braceras countered by stating that she had seen no evidence of the hiring of individuals with backgrounds in Arab languages. She also challenged Mr. Nojeim's assertion that those races and ethnicities are in fact illegitimately targeted based on the evidence. She stated that focusing on a certain group, based on evidence and facts, is not necessarily discriminatory and that law enforcement has to go where the evidence points.[59]

Mr. Shora responded that the Arab American community is in no way endeavoring to destroy America, and that it is rather one of this country's strongest assets in the war against terrorism. He argued that programs such as warrantless surveillance curb this nation's efforts to fight terrorism by targeting the very people who can best aid the government.[60] Commissioner Braceras conceded this may be the case, but asserted that individuals who have attacked our country typically have not been Polish speakers, and thus the FBI is not hiring Polish speakers.[61]

---

[53] Ibid., p. 37.

[54] Ibid., p. 38.

[55] Ibid., pp. 38–39.

[56] Ibid., p. 39.

[57] Ibid., pp. 39–40.

[58] Ibid., p. 40–41.

[59] Ibid., pp. 41–42.

[60] Ibid., p. 42.

[61] Ibid., p. 42.

Commissioner Yaki asked Commissioner Braceras to clarify her position, noting that the FBI is not a foreign intelligence agency, like the Central Intelligence Agency (CIA) or NSA, and is charged with domestic surveillance only. He said that the discussion was based around a domestic program he believed was designed to affect and target members of a community of American citizens. Commissioner Yaki disagreed strongly with Dr. Eastman's interpretation of the *Youngstown* case, contending that later in the opinion Justice Jackson stated that presidential power was not without constitutional limitations. He described the surveillance program as targeting Arab American and Muslim American citizens, and not a group of foreigners on American soil, and asked Dr. Eastman whether he felt this was an incorrect characterization.[62]

Dr. Eastman opined that Commissioner Yaki's description of the surveillance program was incorrect. He pointed to a 1980's hearing in which the Commissioner of the Immigration and Naturalization Service (INS) was asked whether, as the statistics seemed to indicate, a disparate number of Mexican Americans or Hispanics were being targeted at the border. The INS Commissioner indicated that they were not targeting those communities, but were instead targeting drivers of Chevrolet Impalas, which were often used by human smugglers, and that the bulk of people who drove that vehicle through the borders ended up being Hispanic or Mexican American.[63]

Commissioner Yaki took issue with Dr. Eastman's analogy and said it was not applicable. He stated that the situation at hand was akin to targeting people with a Motorola RAZR cell phone, and that it was an invalid assumption to say that, when you tap a phone line, you are simply assuming that it happens to belong to a Muslim American.[64] Dr. Eastman replied that the only trait that will lead to one's phone being tapped under the present program is whether one is talking to a known member of al Qaeda or a group affiliated with al Qaeda. He suggested there was no evidence to indicate Arab Americans were being targeted solely on the basis of race.[65]

Commissioner Yaki said that when there is a database monitoring 550 phone lines at the same time, it is ridiculous to say that there are 550 members of al Qaeda talking all at once.[66] Dr. Eastman responded that there was no evidence that anyone was being targeted based on race as opposed to having ties with terrorist groups.[67]

Commissioner Braceras supported Dr. Eastman, saying that if the INS is making an effort to stop illegal immigration over the Mexican border, by default, most of the people that they stop are going to be Hispanic. She stated that this did not mean that they were being targeted

---

[62] Ibid., pp. 43–44.

[63] Ibid., p. 44.

[64] Ibid., pp. 44–45.

[65] Ibid., pp. 45.

[66] Ibid., p. 45.

[67] Ibid., pp. 45–46.

based on race, but that it was because they were the people most likely to be violating that particular law at that particular point in time.[68]

Commissioner Yaki countered that this was an inapplicable analogy. He stated that the correct situation would be if there were four Hispanic Americans sitting in the room with them and the FBI walked in and asked to talk to those four specifically about being illegal immigrants. He said that border control issues were separate from going into domestic homes and monitoring private conversations without any justification other than the people being monitored are Muslim and Arab Americans.[69]

Commissioner Yaki asked as a matter of procedure whether the Commission had contacted members of the Bush administration to testify at the briefing.[70] Staff Director Marcus said they had.[71] Commissioner Yaki asked what the response had been.[72] Staff Director Marcus said that they had contacted the Office of the Director of National Intelligence and Department of Justice, and that they said that there was very little relating to wiretaps that they could speak of usefully that was not highly classified.[73]

Dr. Eastman suggested that Commissioner Yaki look at whether calls from Swedes into Afghanistan or Iraq are being monitored or not, and whether calls by Arab Americans which are not placed to any targeted members are being monitored. He insisted that there is no evidence to support that either of those scenarios has occurred.[74]

Mr. Nojeim asked the Commission to get individuals from the administration to testify, and to subpoena them if necessary.[75]

Commissioner Kirsanow asked Dr. Eastman about the inherent tension between the authority of the president to use AUMF to engage in this program and the fact that there is a perception that we are not actually at war. Commissioner Kirsanow asserted that we are indeed at war and that the standards for dealing with combatants, not criminals, should apply, although many people did not realize this.[76]

Dr. Eastman agreed that the correct standard was not the criminal standard, but the wartime standard for dealing with enemy combatants. He said that, if people are engaging in war against the United States using nontraditional means, the U.S. must counter using equally nontraditional means. He cited Commissioner Yaki's earlier remarks about the president having to comply with the Fourth Amendment, and said that the correct inquiry was not

---

[68] Ibid., pp. 46–47.

[69] Ibid., p. 47.

[70] Ibid., p. 47.

[71] Ibid., p. 47.

[72] Ibid., p. 48.

[73] Ibid., p. 48.

[74] Ibid., pp. 48–49.

[75] Ibid., p. 49.

[76] Ibid., pp. 49–50.

whether a warrant needed to be sought under the Fourth Amendment, but whether the president's actions were reasonable under the Fourth Amendment during a time of war. Dr. Eastman stressed that the reasonableness of the president's actions had to be considered in the context of a war, and a post-9/11 world when terrorists could use disposable cell phones to initiate an attack.[77]

Mr. Nojeim averred that, whether we called the present situation a war or something else, we must recognize that it is going to stay with us for decades or even generations. He posited that whether we want the president to have the sole discretion to determine if a person should be wiretapped is a question that strikes at the core of who we are as a nation and what we value, and will be an issue that continues beyond the Iraq and Afghanistan conflicts into perpetuity.[78]

Commissioner Braceras agreed with Mr. Nojeim and indicated there were numerous civil rights concerns being raised under the present climate. She indicated however, that these were not concerns the Commission was authorized to address, and stated that the proper inquiry for this forum was not whether the tools should be used at all, but whether there had been discriminatory conduct in their use.[79]

Commissioner Kirsanow raised the concern that one of the possible causes for the January shift in the administration's position (regarding seeking program rather than individual warrants from the FISA courts), is the cumbersome nature of obtaining warrants from FISA. He asked what balance of security and civil liberties would be appropriate in a scenario where New York City might be under threat of attack.[80]

Mr. Nojeim responded that the question of FISA's responsiveness was a non-issue. He cited the emergency provision of FISA that allows government wiretapping for a period of three days prior to obtaining a warrant so long as an application is presented within the three-day period.[81] He also stated that FISA court judges report that they can act quickly, and at times have even responded to government requests at home.[82]

Commissioner Yaki likened the present scenario to when Japanese Americans were interned following the attack on Pearl Harbor. He pointed out that President Roosevelt had exercised his powers under Article 2, and that the Supreme Court had even upheld his authority,[83] even though, according to Commissioner Yaki, no evidence was ever produced of acts of sabotage or disloyalty. Commissioner Yaki raised concerns over condemning an entire community, and said that it would be helpful to know how many people had been subjected to the warrantless wiretapping, and how many of those people were Arabs or Muslims, so as to

---

[77] Ibid., pp. 50–52.

[78] Ibid., pp. 52–53.

[79] Ibid., p. 53.

[80] Ibid., pp. 53–55.

[81] *See* 50 U.S.C. § 1805(e) (2009).

[82] Domestic Wiretapping, Briefing Transcript, pp. 55–56.

[83] *Korematsu v. US*, 323 U.S. 214, 223–24 (1994).

educate the American people about the difference between identifying those who attacked us and those who share the terrorists' ethnicities. By way of example, Commissioner Yaki contended that sweeps were conducted by the FBI of Arab American and Muslim communities during the first Gulf War, an activity he claimed was ended only after public outcry.[84]

Dr. Eastman responded by indicating there was not any evidence the president was targeting people wholesale because of their ethnic or racial background. He asserted this program was not analogous to the internment program of Japanese Americans under President Roosevelt, but was instead a bipartisan effort created by knowledgeable and informed members of Congress. He concluded that simply because a large number of people affected by this program are Muslim does not indicate evidence of discrimination. He stated that the trigger for being wiretapped was whether someone places a call to al Qaeda, not what his or her ethnic background was.[85] Commission Yaki agreed in theory, but said that there was also no evidence to support the position that the call to al Qaeda was the trigger.[86] Commissioner Braceras insisted there was also no evidence to the contrary.[87]

Mr. Shora interjected, calling it irresponsible to assume that only a call to al Qaeda was a trigger. He referenced his earlier example of an individual who was targeted but who made phone calls to a hospital room in a capital city of one of our allies in the Middle East.[88]

Mr. Nojeim said the correct standard to apply was one of individualized suspicion, instead of group suspicion. He asked the Commission to inquire of the administration whether, under the new shift to using FISA courts, the program warrants will require individualized suspicion or not. Mr. Nojeim asserted that Dr. Eastman's analysis that the president has inherent authority is incorrect. He argued the present case is one that fits the third category from Justice Jackson's concurrence in *Youngstown Sheet & Tube*, and is in fact a situation where Congress has acted contrary to what the president seeks. Mr. Nojeim insisted the president's power was at its lowest ebb, and that to assume otherwise would be to illogically presume that Congress, by its silence, authorized the president's program, when in fact it explicitly addressed in FISA the issue of wiretapping individuals in the US.[89]

Commissioner Kirsanow discussed *Youngstown Sheet & Tube* and the FISA emergency contingency pointed out previously by Mr. Nojeim. He asked Mr. Nojeim whether, in reading those two articles of authority together, it was possible that Congress intended to permit the president to engage in this kind of conduct.[90] Mr. Nojeim replied that FISA already contained a wartime provision where the president may wiretap for up to 15 days without a court order. He argued that, if Congress sought to authorize otherwise, it would

---

[84] Ibid., pp. 56–60.

[85] Ibid., pp. 60–61.

[86] Ibid., p. 61.

[87] Ibid., p. 61.

[88] Ibid., pp. 61–62.

[89] Ibid., pp. 62–63.

[90] Ibid., pp. 63–64.

have done so by statute, and cited a Supreme Court case in which the court alluded that Congress does not alter fundamental details of a regulatory scheme in vague terms or ancillary provisions.[91]

Dr. Eastman stated that the same argument had been made in the *Hamdi* case with respect to the Anti-Detention statute. He argued that the Supreme Court held that Congress had, by its silence and through the AUMF, pre-empted the earlier statute. Dr. Eastman noted the Court was capable of doing so because the detention of combatants was central to the war effort, and that, analogously, the ability to monitor enemy communications was equally central to that effort. Dr. Eastman said that, in his opinion, the 6th Circuit would overturn the Michigan District Court's decision outlawing the warrantless wiretapping if they reached the merits of the case.[92]

Mr. Nojeim responded that *Hamdi* involved a battlefield detention, not a domestic issue, and that it would be quite another matter to assert that *Hamdi* authorized domestic spying and domestic wiretapping by the president.[93]

---

[91] Ibid., pp. 64–65. *See Whitman v. American Trucking Ass'n*, 531 U.S. 457 (2001).

[92] Domestic Wiretapping, Briefing Transcript, pp. 65–66. The District Court's decision was overturned. *See* footnote 7.

[93] Ibid., p. 67.

Statements

Note: Statements are unedited by the Commission and are the sole work of the author.

Gregory Nojeim

Associate Director and Chief Legislative Counsel
ACLU Washington Legislative Office

Distinguished members of the Commission—thank you for the opportunity to testify today on behalf of the American Civil Liberties Union regarding the Fourth Amendment, due process and civil rights implications related to the Bush Administration's Terrorist Surveillance Program (TSP). The ACLU is a nonpartisan, nongovernmental organization with hundreds of thousands of members and supporters, and 53 affiliates nationwide.

According to media reports, in 2002 President Bush signed a secret order authorizing the National Security Agency (NSA) to monitor overseas e-mails, telephone calls and other communications – originating within the United States – of hundreds, and perhaps thousands, of U.S. citizens and foreign nationals without first obtaining warrants.[1] The administration subsequently admitted that such warrantless surveillance was occurring and it dubbed it the "Terrorist Surveillance Program." The ACLU believes this program is illegal and unconstitutional and a federal court agrees. We compliment the Commission for holding this briefing to shed additional light on the program, and on the intelligence surveillance that continues today.

It is clear to us that the NSA warrantless spying program violated the Fourth Amendment of the Constitution and federal law. The Fourth Amendment bars unreasonable searches and seizures and requires court approval for such activity except in an emergency. As a diverse group of legal experts—including Judge William Sessions, the former Director of the FBI under President Ronald Reagan—concluded after analyzing all the constitutional and statutory assertions of the administration: "the Justice Department's defense of what it concedes was secret and warrantless electronic surveillance of persons within the United States fails to identify any plausible legal authority for such surveillance."[2]

The U.S. Supreme Court has long held that the conversations of Americans in the U.S. cannot be seized under the Fourth Amendment without court oversight.[3] In a case involving warrantless wiretapping by the Nixon Administration in the name of national security, the Court stressed that "Fourth Amendment freedoms cannot properly be guaranteed if domestic surveillance may be conducted solely within the discretion of the Executive Branch."[4] In that case, the Keith case, the Court reaffirmed that "prior judicial approval is required for the type

---

[1] http://www.washingtonpost.com/wpdyn/content/article/2005/12/16/AR2005121600021.html.

[2] http://www.aclu.org/safefree/nsaspying/24071leg20060109.html.

[3] *Katz v. United States*, 389 U.S. 347 (1967).

[4] *United States v. United States District Court*, 407 U.S. 297 (1972).

of domestic surveillance involved in this case and that such approval may be made in accordance with such reasonable standards as Congress may prescribe."[5]

In the aftermath of Watergate, the United States Senate Select Committee to Study Governmental Operations with Respect to Intelligence Activities (otherwise known as the Church Committee) found that the NSA had unconstitutionally monitored every single international telegram sent or received by American residents or businesses, amounting to millions of telegrams.[6] At that time, Congress determined that through the NSA's warrantless surveillance programs, the NSA alone had created specific files on approximately 75,000 United States citizens, and eavesdropped on journalists, Members of Congress and their spouses, and other government officials. Congress found that the NSA had also created a watch list of Americans who were suspected of foreign influence merely because they opposed a foreign war – including ordinary Americans who belonged to the Quaker church, as well as celebrities such as Joan Baez and Dr. Benjamin Spock.[7] The Church Committee found that in the absence of any judicial check, the executive branch had spied on government employees, journalists, anti-war activists and others for political purposes.

In response in part to the findings of the Church Committee, Congress passed the comprehensive Foreign Intelligence Surveillance Act (FISA) to provide the "exclusive" authority for the wiretapping of US persons in investigations to protect national security.[8] As the Senate Report noted, FISA "was designed . . . to curb the practice by which the Executive Branch may conduct warrantless electronic surveillance on its own unilateral determination that national security justifies it."[9] Under FISA, federal agents are required to get court approval in order to monitor the communications of any person in the United States. FISA does permit the surveillance of people in the country linked to national security threats, but only with a court order. FISA provides that no one may engage in electronic surveillance "except as authorized by statute," and it specifies civil and criminal penalties for electronic surveillance undertaken without statutory authority.

By failing to follow the exclusive provisions of FISA and Title III governing wiretaps of Americans, the warrantless NSA wiretapping program violated both the Fourth Amendment and the letter and spirit of the federal law passed to protect and vindicate privacy rights.

Without court oversight, one cannot be sure that innocent people's everyday communications are not monitored or catalogued by the NSA or other agencies. During the Cold War, the list of people considered by McCarthy to be "communists" was long and it was wrong in many notable instances. In the 1960s, J. Edgar Hoover secretly wiretapped the communications of

---

[5] Id. at 324. Of course, the Keith case is not directly on point because the NSA's warrantless surveillance involves interception of conversations between a person in the U.S. and a person abroad, as opposed to wholly domestic conversations.

[6] "Intelligence Activities and the Rights of Americans," Final Report of the Select Committee to Study Governmental Operations with Respect to Intelligence Activities, United States Senate, Book III (National Security Surveillance Affecting Americans).

[7] James Bamford, "Big Brother Is Listening," the Atlantic Monthly, pp. 65-70, April 2006.

[8] 18 U.S.C. § 2511(2)(f).

[9] S. Rep. No. 95-604(I), at 7, 1978 U.S.C.C.A.N. 3904, 3908.

the leader of the civil rights movement, the Reverend Dr. Martin Luther King Jr., under the guise of national security. And President Nixon personally approved wiretaps of cabinet members, government employees, journalists and other Americans he didn't like or didn't trust. These and other revelations led to the passage of FISA to protect Americans' Fourth Amendment right to privacy in their conversations by requiring judicial oversight of all US wiretaps including those in the name of national security.

Unfortunately, the government has a lengthy track record post 9-11 track record of pursuing ineffective anti-terrorist dragnets that intrude on innocent Americans' rights. Examples include certain airline passenger identity screening programs and the now-outlawed Total Information Awareness data-mining program. Other examples include disclosures that FBI or Defense Department agents are spying on Quakers and other pacifists, environmentalists, and vegetarians, the opening of Americans' mail without a warrant, and revelations that the Pentagon and CIA are using "National Security Letters" without oversight or judicial approval to collect the financial records of Americans – all in the name of national security. Without a judicial check, the powerful electronic surveillance tools of the NSA can be trained on anyone.

The administration has repeatedly stated that the president is "mindful" of Americans' civil liberties, but our system of government requires checks on power, not deference to those in power. The administration also claims that the Authorization for the Use of Military Force (AUMF) passed by Congress on September 18, 2001 authorized the warrantless NSA surveillance program. Yet there is no evidence that Congress intended to override FISA in passing the AUMF.

In fact, within 40 days of the vote on the AUMF, Congress enacted 25 changes to FISA at the request of President Bush in the USA PATRIOT Act (Title II, including Section 215 relating to getting court approval for business or library records as well as Section 206 regarding getting court approval for multiple-point wiretaps), but none of these amendments struck the requirement that the president get judicial approval to conduct electronic surveillance of people in the U.S. Congress has made other changes to FISA in the past four years.[10] This legislative history only serves to reinforce the continuing legal obligation of the administration to follow FISA regardless of the AUMF.

ACLU Legal Action

On January 17, 2006, the ACLU filed a lawsuit in Michigan on behalf of prominent journalists, scholars, attorneys, and national nonprofit organizations whose work requires them to communicate by telephone and e-mail with people outside the United States, including people in the Middle East and Asia.[11] Because of the nature of their calls and e-mails, and the identities and locations of those with whom they communicate, the plaintiffs

---

[10] Pub. L. No. 107-56, 115 Stat. 272 (2001).

[11] The clients in the case include the American Civil Liberties Union; the Council on American-Islamic Relations (CAIR); the National Association of Criminal Defense Lawyers; Greenpeace; James Bamford, author; Larry Diamond, senior fellow at the Hoover Institution; Christopher Hitchens, author and reporter; and Tara McKelvey, senior editor at The American Prospect.

have a well-founded belief that the NSA is intercepting their communications. The NSA program is disrupting the ability of these groups and individuals to talk with sources, locate witnesses, conduct scholarship and engage in advocacy.

By seriously compromising the free speech and privacy rights of the plaintiffs and all Americans, the ACLU charges that the NSA program violates the First and Fourth Amendments of the United States Constitution. The program authorizes the NSA to intercept the private communications of people who the government has no reason to believe have committed, or are planning to commit, any crime without first obtaining a warrant or prior judicial approval. The ACLU also charges that the program violates the constitutional principle of separation of powers because President Bush authorized it in excess of his Executive authority and contrary to limits imposed by Congress.

The government responded to the lawsuit by arguing that the case should be dismissed under the state secrets privilege, meaning the program was so secret and so sensitive that not even a federal court could review what was happening and whether it violated the law.

On August 17, 2006, U.S. District Court Judge Anna Diggs Taylor refused to dismiss the challenge to the wiretapping program under the state secrets privilege. She ruled the NSA program violates the First Amendment, the Fourth Amendment, and the Foreign Intelligence Surveillance Act. "It was never the intent of the Framers to give the President such unfettered control," Taylor wrote in the decision, "particularly where his actions blatantly disregard the parameters clearly enumerated in the Bill of Rights."[12] The government appealed that ruling.

The appeals were heard on January 31, 2007, before Judges Alice Batchelder, Ronald Gilman and Julia Gibbons of the United States Court of Appeals for the Sixth Circuit Court.[13] A decision is pending.

Telecommunications Companies and the NSA

In May 2006, USA Today revealed that since shortly after 9/11 at least two major phone companies—AT&T and Verizon—have been voluntarily granting the NSA direct, mass access to their customers' calling records, and that the NSA had compiled a giant database of those records. Subsequently confirmed by 19 lawmakers, this program extends to all Americans, not just those suspected of terrorist or criminal activity.

According to media reports, the goal of this program is to "create a database of every call ever made" within the nation's borders.[14] This information can easily be linked to determine a person's identity, friends and interests.

---

[12] http://www.aclu.org/pdfs/safefree/nsamemo.opinion.judge.taylor.081706.pdf.

[13] The ACLU was supported by a number of organizations who filed an amicus brief, including the National Association for the Advancement of Colored People, the American-Arab Anti-Discrimination Committee, the Asian American Legal Defense and Education Fund, Japanese Americans Citizens League, and the League of United Latin American Citizens, among others.

[14] http://www.usatoday.com/news/washington/2006-05-10-nsa_x.htm.

The unauthorized sharing of phone records is illegal under both state and federal law. As with the NSA's program of wiretapping on Americans' conversations and e-mail, the president has evoked the threat of terrorism and used a convoluted interpretation of presidential power to ignore the law. That means the NSA is operating outside the law—and without independent review by Congress or outside regulators.

In an effort to expose the depth of the NSA's unlawful wiretapping, the ACLU has filed complaints with the Public Utility Commissions (PUCs) in 24 states to trigger investigations into whether AT&T and/or Verizon have provided the NSA with their customers' phone records. Without revealing secret information, utility commissions have the power and the legal obligation to learn what the phone companies are doing with their customers' private information and whether they are being upfront with their customers about those practices.

In Maine, Connecticut, Vermont and Missouri the government filed federal lawsuits to prevent the PUCs from investigating the program. The government also filed a separate lawsuit in New Jersey to stop subpoenas about the program. The phone companies, in conjunction with the federal government, have moved to consolidate and transfer all of the cases to California. More than 40 cases posing challenges to telephone companies' use of consumer data in compliance with the NSA's program have already been consolidated in California, including the Maine lawsuit. The ACLU of Illinois and the ACLU of Northern California originally brought two of the cases.

Additionally, the Maine Public Utilities Commission had initiated contempt proceedings against Verizon Maine for failure to comply with an August 9 order by the Commission. The order required a Verizon official to swear under oath to the truth of previous statements issued by the company stating it did not give customer records to the NSA. In February the US District Court of Maine, citing national security concerns, ruled that the Maine PUC cannot compel Verizon to disclose whether the telephone company participated in the warrantless domestic surveillance program.

Claims the New Surveillance Program Now Complies with FISA

In January 2007, the Bush administration announced that it had abandoned its warrantless wiretapping program in favor of a new program it did not describe that is subject to FISA court approval. Unfortunately the administration is still claiming the President has the "inherent authority" to engage in warrantless eavesdropping,[15] and nothing would stop the administration from resuming warrantless surveillance at any time. But it is clear that the inherent powers of the president do not include the ability to conduct a warrantless, indefinite and unlimited domestic surveillance campaign that is expressly prohibited by law.

The process used to get the new program approved by a FISA court judge created a number of questions that need to be answered. For example, why did it take two years to get the approval of just one of the fifteen FISA judges? Were other judges approached to approve the program? What kind of "innovative arrangement" was used to obtain approval? And to

---

[15] http://www.pbs.org/newshour/bb/law/jan-june07/gonzales_01-19.html.

what extent will the government release information to the public that will help legal scholars ascertain whether the order complies with the requirements of FISA?

It is not yet clear as to whether the government is now getting individualized warrants based on individual suspicion, or "program warrants" that do not require individualized suspicion of wrongdoing. Both FISA and the Fourth Amendment require warrants be based on individual suspicion. The Bush administration has strongly advocated for legislation that would allow the use of program warrants, and the Justice Department has said it came up with an "innovative arrangement" to get the program approved. But there are questions as to whether this process used will survive legal and constitutional scrutiny. We have yet to see other than conclusive documents from the administration describing the new program and how it complies with federal law and the Constitution.

Program warrants (also known as general warrants) were one of the reasons Americans fought the Revolutionary War and are specifically prohibited by the framers of the Constitution in the Fourth Amendment. Certainly no one could suggest that our nation's founders would approve of program warrants.

With a program warrant, agents are more likely to eavesdrop on conversations that do not involve a person legitimately targeted for surveillance. In other words, the net they cast is unconstitutionally wide. The purpose of the Fourth Amendment is to focus any investigative intrusion on the wrongdoer. Yet program warrants raise the possibility of an unfocussed intrusion on many people, possibly affecting countless individuals who have done nothing wrong and are not agents of foreign powers.

Furthermore, the administration's claim that the new program now complies with FISA does not pardon those responsible for five years of lawless surveillance. In fact, this assertion raises serious questions as to why the government had not complied with FISA in the first place.

Conclusion

The ACLU believes that both privacy and security can be successfully pursued and that privacy need not be sacrificed for security. We believe that both need to be maximized. For almost 30 years FISA has been successfully protecting both privacy and security.

The Fourth Amendment was specifically enshrined in the Constitution to prevent the type of warrantless surveillance the President and the NSA have engaged in, and current law requires that judicially approved wiretaps under Title III or FISA provide the "exclusive" authority for wiretapping Americans in this country. FISA is a criminal statute. When warrantless wiretapping outside of FISA was conducted, a crime was committed.[16] One way to protect civil rights of Americans and ensure that this type of illegal and unconstitutional behavior does not happen again is to hold accountable those responsible for five years of lawbreaking.

---

[16] 18 U.S.C. § 2511(2)(f); see also 50 U.S.C. § 1809 (making it a crime to wiretap Americans without a court order under the guise of national security or other rationales).

The administration's lack of disclosure about both the warrantless surveillance program and the new program has been one of the most troubling aspects of this process. Clearly, full oversight and transparency are needed to ensure that the new domestic surveillance program is addressing civil rights and due process concerns. The documents that justify the program should be made available consistent with national security needs, and independent Constitutional scholars should scrutinize them.

It is evident that the government has gathered information illegally, but has not disclosed whether, or how, it will minimize the damage that has been done. This means that audits will also be required to make certain that illegally gathered information is not being used— including all information gathered through the warrantless surveillance program.

We commend the Commission for holding this briefing. As part of its oversight function and statutory duty to appraise the Federal government's administration of justice, we ask that the Commission conduct formal hearings into the program and that the Commission recommend that Congress do the same.

In holding additional hearings on this matter, we would ask that the Commission, if necessary, use its authority to issue subpoenas and interrogatories to the appropriate government agencies in order to shed much needed light onto the government's actions. At the conclusion of its investigation, we are hopeful the Commission will recommend in any forthcoming report that Congress find out how many Americans have had their privacy violated through the surveillance programs, what has been done with the information collected and how it is being used.

The Commission should also recommend that Congress investigate the administration's claims that the program now operates under the supervision of the FISA Court, and that the administration is upholding the letter and spirit of the law. Congress must find out who is responsible for the decision to break the law and hold them accountable. And in that respect, the Commission should recommend that Congress consider how best to ensure that this and future presidents stay within the bounds of the Constitution. It is critical that lawmakers uphold their responsibility to the Constitution and the American people and conduct a thorough inquiry.

John Eastman

Henry Salvatori Professor of Law & Community Service
Chapman University School of Law
Director of the Center for Constitutional Jurisprudence, The Claremont Institute

Listening to the Enemy: The President's Power to Conduct Surveillance of Enemy Communications During Time of War

Ever since the New York Times published classified information in December 2005[1] about the efforts by the National Security Agency to intercept enemy communications to or from sources in the United States (as authorized by the President in his capacity as Commander-In-Chief), there has been a great hue and cry about the President's "illegal" conduct. Calls of impeachment have even been heard, both in the media[2] and in the halls of Congress.[3] The Congressional Research Service ("CRS") weighed in at the request of members of Congress,[4] concluding that "it might be argued" that the President had violated the Foreign Intelligence Surveillance Act ("FISA"),[5] a statute adopted by Congress in the late 1970s. In stark contrast, the President, backed by a lengthy legal analysis by the Department of Justice,[6] defended both the legality and the necessity of the NSA surveillance program to the overall war against terrorism.

The current controversy over the President's surveillance program, like the controversies over the Boland Amendment in the 1980s, the War Powers Act in the 1970s, and countless other statutory efforts by Congress to limit the President's executive powers, forces us to give serious consideration to the Founders' constitutional design. In particular, it is important to assess the strength of the competing analyses provided by the Congressional Research Service and the Department of Justice with respect to whether the President's actions "violated" FISA and, if so, whether the FISA, so interpreted, would be an unconstitutional intrusion upon powers that the Constitution confers directly upon the President.

It is perhaps no surprise that the CRS report sided with congressional power, while the DOJ report sides with the President. CRS rightly touts itself as the policy arm of the Congress, and it is answerable to Congress for its work. Similarly, the Department of Justice is an executive Department, answerable to the President; indeed, Article II of the Constitution specifically authorizes the President to require the opinion, in writing, of the principal officer of each

---

[1] James Risen and Eric Lichtblau, "Bush Lets U.S. Spy on Callers Without Courts," New York Times (Dec. 16, 2005).

[2] See, e.g., Elizabeth Holtzman, "The Impeachment of George W. Bush," *The Nation* (Jan. 30, 2006)

[3] See, e.g., H. Res. 635 (introduced Dec. 18, 2005, by Rep. Conyers).

[4] Elizabeth B. Bazan and Jennifer K. Elsea, Congressional Research Memorandum, "Presidential Authority to Conduct Warrantless Electronic Surveillance to Gather Foreign Intelligence Information" (Jan. 5, 2006) ("CRS Report").

[5] 50 U.S.C. §§ 1801-1862 (2000 & Supp. II 2002).

[6] U.S. Department of Justice, "Legal Authorities Supporting the Activities of the National Security Agency Described by the President" (Jan. 19. 2006) ("DOJ Report").

executive department. While both entities have well-deserved reputations for generally providing unbiased assessments to their superiors, we would be remiss not to notice where their institutional allegiances lie. As Chief Justice (and former President) Taft noted eighty years ago in *Myers v. United States*,[7] "[e]ach head of a department is and must be the President's alter ego in the matters of that department where the president is required by law to exercise authority." The Supreme Court has recently recognized, even more forcefully, that the same is true for agents of the Legislature: "In constitutional terms, [Congress's] removal powers over the Comptroller General's office dictate that he will be *subservient* to Congress."[8] What was true of the Comptroller General in *Bowsher* is equally true of the Congressional Research Service, which is statutorily designated as an "agent" of Congress and its committees.[9] Although the CRS is legally obliged to conduct its work "without partisan bias,"[10] there is no similar prohibition on institutional bias, and CRS is clearly a creature of Congress, "discharging its responsibilities to Congress," "rendering to Congress the most effective and efficient service," and "responding most expeditiously, effectively, and efficiently to the special needs of Congress."[11] The CRS report itself acknowledges that it was prepared in response to requests from "more than one congressional *client*,"[12] and that role as advocate for its congressional clients is made amply clear throughout the report, which defends Congress's efforts through FISA to "put[] to rest the notion that Congress recognizes an inherent Presidential power to conduct" foreign intelligence surveillance within the United States.[13]

However much some members of Congress might prefer the conclusions reached in the CRS Report to those reached by the DOJ, therefore, protecting as they do congressional prerogatives at the expense of the Executive, the DOJ's conclusions are much better grounded in constitutional text, precedent, history, and the political theory espoused by our nation's Founders than those reached by the authors of the CRS Report.

The argument that existing precedent supports the President's position is particularly compelling. The two landmark cases that mark the poles of Supreme Court precedent addressing the interplay between the Executive and the Congress on matters of foreign policy and war are *Youngstown Sheet and Tube Co. v. Sawyer*,[14] and *United States v. Curtiss-Wright Export Corp.*[15] In *Youngstown*, the Supreme Court rebuffed President Truman's efforts to seize the nation's steel mills in order to secure the ready supply of steel for the military conflict then underway in Korea, and there is language in the case favorable to proponents of congressional power. In *Curtiss-Wright*, on the other hand, the Supreme Court articulated a very broad theory of presidential power in the foreign-policy arena which remains valid to

---

[7] 272 U.S. 52 (1926).

[8] *Bowsher v. Synar*, 478 U.S. 714, 730 (1986) (emphasis added).

[9] 2 U.S.C. § 166(d)(1)(C).

[10] *Id.* § 166(d).

[11] *Id.* § 166(b)(1)(A-C).

[12] CRS Report, p.1, footer (emphasis added).

[13] *Id.* at 17.

[14] 343 U.S. 579 (1952).

[15] 299 U.S. 304 (1936).

this day, acknowledging that "[t]he President is the sole organ of the nation in its external relations, and its sole representative with foreign nations."[16]

Not surprisingly, given its institutional affiliation, the CRS Report begins its analysis with the *Youngstown* case (and particularly with Justice Jackson's concurring opinion in that case), bolstered by a pro-Congress interpretive gloss placed on the case by a district court decision in *United States v. Andonian*.[17] Yet the CRS Report fails to give adequate play to what it calls the "nuances" of Justice Jackson's important concurring opinion in the case, treating the case as much more solicitous of congressional power than it actually is.

Justice Jackson famously described a three-tiered system for assessing the separation of powers issues that lie at the intersection of presidential and congressional power. Obviously, the President's authority is at its peak when he acts both pursuant to his own authority under the Constitution and by virtue of additional statutory authority given to him by Congress— Justice Jackson's Category 1. Less strong, but no less certain, is when the President acts by virtue of his own constitutional powers, in the face of congressional silence—Category 2. Finally, Justice Jackson even conceded that, at times, the President could act pursuant to his Article II constitutional powers despite an explicit act of Congress to the contrary—Category 3. Congress cannot pass a law that curtails powers the President has directly from the Constitution itself. The problem for Truman, according to Justice Jackson, was not that he exceeded statutory authority, but that his constitutional war powers did not, *under the circumstances*, permit him to trump the mechanisms of the relevant congressional statute. Congress had not authorized the war, and the nation's steel mills were too far removed from the "theater of war" to fall under the President's power as Commander-in-Chief.

Contrary to the conclusions drawn by the CRS, a careful review of the *Youngstown* holding in general, and of Justice Jackson's concurring opinion in particular, yields several important distinctions that vindicate President Bush's latest actions in the war against terrorism. First, in the Authorization for Use of Military Force ("AUMF") that it adopted a week after the terrorist attacks on September 11, 2001, Congress *did* authorize the use of force in terms broad enough to permit the President's actions.[18] In *Hamdi v. Rumsfeld,*[19] the Supreme Court held that the AUMF statute was broad enough to give the President authority to detain U.S. citizens as enemy combatants even though such detentions were not explicitly authorized (and but for the AUMF would be prohibited by another statute, 18 U.S.C. § 4001(a)); surely it is therefore broad enough to serve as authority for the much lesser intrusion on personal liberty at issue with surveillance of international calls made to or received from our enemies. As such, the President's actions at issue here fall into Justice Jackson's first category, in which the President's power is at its zenith; the DOJ Report's analysis on this point is much more persuasive than the CRS Report's analysis.

---

[16] 299 U.S., at 319 (international quotation marks and citations omitted).

[17] 735 F. Supp. 1469 (C.D. Cal. 1990), *aff'd and remanded on other grounds*, 29 F.3d 634 (9th Cir. 1994), *cert. denied,* 513 U.S. 1128 (1995).

[18] Authorization for Use of Military Force, Pub. L. No. 107-40, § 2(a), 115 Stat. 224, 224 (Sept. 18, 2001).

[19] 542 U.S. 507 (2004).

Second, as September 11 made very clear, the United States *is* a "theater of war," and the full panoply of presidential powers in time of war comes into play—his power as Commander-in-Chief; his power as the nation's top executive; and his inherent power as the organ of U.S. sovereignty on the world stage. This is more than simply a "point of view" that "*might* be argued," as the CRS Report states.[20] The agents of our stateless, terrorist enemies are here on U.S. soil, aiming to strike at our infrastructure, our citizens, and our very way of life at every possible opportunity. Thus, even if the AUMF was not sufficient to sustain the President's executive order, and even if FISA is read as an attempt by Congress to circumscribe the President's own constitutional powers, Justice Jackson recognized that in such a conflict, Congress could not by statute restrict powers that the President has directly from Article II of the Constitution. Congress itself recognized this in the AUMF, when it noted that "the President has authority *under the Constitution* to take action to deter and prevent acts of international terrorism against the United States . . . ."[21] The AUMF preamble reflects the view of Congress itself prior to the adoption of FISA, when it expressly recognized the "constitutional power of the President to take such measures as he deems necessary to protect the Nation against actual or potential attack . . ., [and] to obtain foreign intelligence information deemed essential to the security of the United States. . . ."[22]

But whether or not the CRS Report misreads Justice Jackson's concurring opinion from *Youngstown*, most troubling about the CRS analysis is that it does not grapple with the *Curtiss-Wright* case at all, citing it only once, deep in a footnote, and then only in a parenthetical quotation from a lower court decision.[23] Any neutral assessment of the important separation of powers questions at issue here warranted a thorough consideration of *Curtiss-Wright* and the theory of presidential power it recognized (as well as the even more long-standing precedent on which the decision in *Curtiss-Wright* relied, including *The Prize Cases*[24]), yet none is to be found in the CRS Report. Instead, every indulgence in favor of congressional authority that can even weakly be drawn from existing judicial opinions is drawn, and every recognition by the courts of inherent executive power is downplayed or ignored.

Nowhere is the CRS's slant toward Congress more manifest than in the Report's discussion of the FISA Court of Review's decision in *In re Sealed Case*, which expressly stated: "We take for granted that the President does have [inherent authority to conduct warrantless searches to obtain foreign intelligence information], and, assuming that is so, *FISA could not encroach on the President's constitutional power*."[25] Instead of acknowledging the import of this unbelievably clear statement, the CRS Report begrudgingly finds in it only "some support" for the President's position, and even then finds the scope of the support "to be a matter with respect to which there are differing views."[26]

---

[20] CRS Report at 37.

[21] AUMF, Preamble, PL 107-40, 115 Stat. 224 (Sept. 18, 2001) (emphasis added).

[22] 82 Stat. 214, formerly codified at 18 U.S.C. § 2511(3).

[23] CRS Report, at 31 n. 104 (citing *United States v. Truong Dinh Hung*, 629 F.2d 908, 914 (4th Cir. 1980)).

[24] 67 U.S. (2 Black) 635 (1863).

[25] 310 F.3d 717 (U.S. Foreign Intell. Surveillance Ct. Rev. 2002) (emphasis added).

[26] CRS Report at 33.

The DOJ Report, in contrast, fully grapples with the competing cases and provides a well-reasoned analysis for its proposition that the cases clearly support the inherent constitutional authority of a President to conduct surveillance of communications from or to enemies of the United States and their supporters in time of war. Almost by default, then, the DOJ Report makes the stronger case, but even where the CRS Report does take up the debate by way of its discussion of lower court decisions, the CRS Report's authors are hard-pressed to find in the existing precedent support for the proposition that the President does not have inherent authority to conduct the surveillances at issue here. The best they can muster is that "*it might be argued* that the President's asserted inherent authority to engage warrantless electronic surveillance was . . . limited" by Congress's adoption of FISA, and that the reliance by the FISA Court of Review in *In re Sealed Case* on pre-FISA cases "as a basis for its assumption of the continued vitality of the President's inherent constitutional authority to authorize warrantless electronic surveillance for the purpose of gathering foreign intelligence information *might be viewed* as *somewhat* undercutting the persuasive force of the Court of Review's statement."[27] This is a classic wiggle by lawyers trying to reach the conclusion favored by their clients in the face of precedent that is squarely against them.

Curtiss-Wright provides powerful support for the President's position. In that case, adopting the views expressed by John Marshall while serving in Congress prior to his appointment as Secretary of State and ultimately as Chief Justice of the United States, the Supreme Court recognized that "[t]he President is the sole organ of the nation in its external relations, and its sole representative with foreign nations."[28] As "sole organ" in the foreign affairs arena, the President has inherent constitutional authority—indeed, the constitutional duty[29]—to conduct surveillance of communications with enemies of the United States and people he reasonable believes to be working with them, in order to prevent attacks against the United States. Were FISA to be interpreted in such a fashion as to restrict the President's power in this arena, it may well be unconstitutional—something that the FISA drafters themselves recognized.[30] Congress cannot by mere statute restrict powers that the President holds directly from the Constitution itself. John Marshall's 1800 statement to Congress dealt with an attempt by Congress to circumscribe the President's powers in the negotiation of treaties, much like the interpretations of the FISA statute being pushed by some in Congress is an attempt to circumscribe the President's power to conduct foreign intelligence surveillance, yet the Supreme Court in *Curtiss-Wright* was manifestly clear that Congress had no authority to intrude upon the President's constitutional powers in the foreign arena: "Into the field of negotiation [of treaties] the Senate cannot intrude; and Congress itself is powerless to invade it."[31]

It should be noted that this Administration is not the first to make such claims. Indeed, as the DOJ Report correctly notes, similar arguments have been advanced, successfully, by every

---

[27] CRS Report, at 32 (emphasis added).

[28] 299 U.S., at 319 (citing Annals, 6th Cong., col. 613 (Mar. 7, 1800) (statement of Rep. Marshall).

[29] *See* U.S. Const. art. IV, § 4; *The Prize Cases*, 67 U.S. (2 Black) 635, 638 (1863).

[30] *See* H.R. Conf. Rep. No. 95-1720, at 35, *reprinted in* 1978 U.S.C.C.A.N. 4048, 4064.

[31] *Curtiss-Wright*, 299 U.S., at 319.

administration since electronic surveillance technology was developed. The notion that Congress cannot by mere statute truncate powers the President holds directly from the Constitution is a common feature of executive branch communications with the Congress. Two examples from the DOJ Report are particularly revealing: Griffin Bell, President Jimmy Carter's Attorney General, testified during debate in Congress over the adoption of FISA that, although FISA did not recognize any inherent power of the President, it "does not take away the power [of] the President under the Constitution."[32] President Clinton's Deputy Attorney General, Jamie Gorelick, made a similar point while testifying before Congress when amendments to FISA were being considered in 1994: "[T]he Department of Justice believes, and the case law supports, that the President has inherent authority to conduct warrantless physical searches for foreign intelligence purposes . . . ."[33]

Granted, some may think this analysis affords too much power to the President; but their beef is with the drafters of our Constitution, not with the current President who, following the example of a good number of his predecessors, has determined it necessary to exercise the full extent of his constitutional powers in order to defend our nation against attack. Our nation's Founders created a "unitary executive" (that is, an executive branch headed by a single person rather than a committee, who is responsible for the actions of the entire executive branch and accountable primarily and directly to the people, not to Congress), strong enough to protect "the community against foreign attacks," with "secrecy" and "dispatch" if necessary.[34] And it made the Executive largely independent of the Legislature, particularly in the foreign policy arena. As the Supreme Court noted in *Bowsher*, "unlike parliamentary systems, the President, under Article II, is responsible not to the Congress but to the people, subject only to impeachment proceedings which are exercised by the two Houses as representatives of the people."[35] Indeed, the Court in *Bowsher* correctly recognized that the real concern of the Founders was with Legislative usurpation of Executive power, not the other way around. "The dangers of congressional usurpation of Executive Branch functions have long been recognized," it noted. "'[T]he debates of the Constitutional Convention, and the Federalist Papers, are replete with expressions of fear that the Legislative Branch of the National Government will aggrandize itself at the expense of the other two branches.'"[36]

Thus, while it may be tempting to some to follow the conclusions reached by the CRS Report rather than the much better reasoned and more thoroughly-documented conclusions drawn by the Department of Justice, they do so at the expense of the constitutional design bequeathed to us by our Founders, a design which has worked magnificently well in protecting both our nation's security and our individual liberties for over two centuries. Under the Constitution,

---

[32] DOJ Report at 8 (citing Foreign Intelligence Electronic Surveillance Act of 1978: Hearings on H.R. 5764, H.R. 9745, H.R. 7308, and H.R. 5632 Before the Subcomm. on Legislation of the House Comm. on Intelligence, 95th Cong., 2d Sess. 15 (1978) (Statement of Attorney General Bell)).

[33] DOJ Report at 8 (citing "Amending the Foreign Intelligence Surveillance Act: Hearings Before the House Permanent Select Comm. On Intelligence, 103d Cong. 2d Sess. 61 (1994) (statement of Deputy Attorney General Jamie S. Gorelick)).

[34] The Federalist, No. 70, at 424 (Clinton Rossiter, ed., 1961).

[35] 478 U.S., at 722.

[36] *Id.*, at 727 (citing *Buckley v. Valeo*, 424 U.S. 1, 129 (1976)).

confirmed by two centuries of historical practice and ratified by Supreme Court precedent, the President clearly has the authority to conduct surveillance of enemy communications in time of war and of the communications to and from those he reasonably believes are affiliated with our enemies. Moreover, it should go without saying that such activities are a fundamental incident of war, particularly in a war such as this where the battle for intelligence is not only the front line but in many respects the most significant front in the war. The Authorization for the Use of Military Force, therefore, must be viewed as lending Congress's own support to the constitutional powers directly conferred on the President by Article II. Some may wish to question the wisdom of the President's surveillance activities— I happen to think the necessity of them will be borne out in the fullness of time—but we should not confuse such a dispute over tactics and policy with the present dispute over the constitutional authority of the President to undertake them.

* * *

That conclusion puts the New York Times disclosure of the NSA's classified surveillance program into stark relief. No one contests that classified information was illegally provided to the Times and then subsequently published by it. And to my knowledge, no one seriously contends that the individuals who leaked the information are not subject to prosecution for violating the Espionage Act[37] (or even subject to prosecution for treason if it could be proved that their intent in leaking the classified information was to undermine our war effort and thereby give aid and comfort to the enemy).[38]

Even those who would seek to bestow on the leaker the protected status of "whistle-blower" surely will acknowledge that the whistle-blower statute requires that the allegedly illegal activities be reported internally, through a certain specified administrative route, rather than shouted to the world from the front pages of our nation's major newspapers.[39] Otherwise, the whistle-blower statute would permit every government employee to be a classified information law unto himself, determining what should or should not be secret. The devastating consequences to our national security, and also to individual privacy, of such a flawed interpretation should be manifest.

But what of the liability of the New York Times itself? Is it equally subject to the prohibitions of the Espionage Act? In May 2006, Bill Keller, Executive Editor of the New York Times, published an important letter to the editors of the Wall Street Journal challenging the notion "that when presidents declare that secrecy is in the national interest, reporters should take that at face value." Implicit in his rejection of that proposition is the view that reporters generally, and perhaps the editors of the New York Times in particular, are free to ignore the laws regarding publication of classified information when, *in their view*, the benefit to the public from gaining access to the information would outweigh any harm that might flow from its disclosure. Keller elaborated:

---

[37] 18 U.S.C. §972 et seq.; *see also, e.g., United States v. Morison*, 604 F. Supp. 655 (D.C. Md.), *appeal dismissed*, 774 F.2d 1156 (4th Cir. 1985).

[38] U.S. Const. Art. III, § 3, cl. 1; *Tomoya Kawakita v. United States*, 343 U.S. 717 (1952); *Cramer v. United States*, 325 U.S. 1 (1945).

[39] See The Intelligence Community Whistleblower Protection Act of 1998, 50 U.S.C. § 403q.

> [P]residents are entitled to a respectful and attentive hearing, particularly when they make claims based on the safety of the country. In the case of the eavesdropping story, President Bush and other figures in his administration were given abundant opportunities to explain why they felt our information should not be published. We considered the evidence presented to us, agonized over it, delayed publication because of it. In the end, their case did not stand up to the evidence our reporters amassed, and we judged that the responsible course was to publish what we knew and let readers assess it themselves.

This is truly an extraordinary claim, that somehow the New York Times is entitled to weigh evidence and determine for itself whether to publish classified information—in other words, that the New York Times is above the law and can publish whatever classified information it sees fit, with impunity.

Section 798 of the Espionage Act makes no such exception, of course. Its text is unambiguous. "Whoever knowingly and willfully . . . publishes . . . any classified information . . . concerning the communication activities of the United States . . . Shall be fined not more than $10,000 or imprisoned not more than ten years, or both."[40] Subsection (b) of the Act defines "communication intelligence" as "all procedures and methods used in the interception of communications and the obtaining of information from such communications by other than the intended recipient." In the cloak and dagger world of intelligence gathering, this statutory prohibition is a model of clarity—it is illegal to publish classified information about our intelligence-gathering efforts and capabilities.

Keller and other defenders of his claimed exemption from this legal mandate point to the Pentagon Papers case, *New York Times Co. v. United States*,[41] as support for the proposition that the media's publication of classified intelligence communications information is protected by the First Amendment. There are two fundamental flaws with that contention.[42] First, the Pentagon Papers case dealt only with a request for an injunction, or prior restraint, on publication—the quintessential restriction on the freedom of the press in mind of those who drafted and ratified the Bill of Rights. But five Justices in that case (Chief Justice Burger and Justices White, Stewart, Harlan, and Blackmun), recognized what our nation's founders also understood—a prohibition on prior restraints does not eliminate liability for post-publication prosecution for abuses of the freedom. Justice White, for example, joined by Justice Stewart, specifically noted in his concurring opinion that "a responsible press may choose never to publish the more sensitive materials" "because of the hazards of criminal sanctions."[43] Justice Harlan, joined by Chief Justice Burger and Justice Blackmun, would have required full briefing and consideration of whether an injunction was proper in light of

---

[40] 18 U.S.C. § 798(a)(3).

[41] 403 U.S. 713 (1971).

[42] There is also a third, more minor flaw, in reliance on the Pentagon Papers case. The information that the government sought to enjoin the New York Times and Washington Post from publishing was governed by Section 793(e) of the Espionage Act, 18 U.S.C. § 793(e), not Section 798, which applies to the intelligence communications information at issue here. As Justice Douglas noted in his concurring opinion, Section 793(e) barred only the "communication" of classified information relating to the national defense, unlike Section 798, which bars both the publication and communication of signals communication information, demonstrating (at least for Justice Douglas) "that Congress was capable of and did distinguish between publishing and communication in the various sections of the Espionage Act."

[43] 403 U.S., at 733.

the "doctrine against enjoining conduct in violation of criminal statutes."[44] James Wilson made this same point during the Pennsylvania ratifying convention in December 1787:

> I presume it was not in the view of the honorable gentleman to say there is no such thing as a libel, or that the writers of such ought not to be punished. The idea of the liberty of the press is not carried so far as this in any country. What is meant by the liberty of the press is, that there should be no antecedent restraint upon it; but that every author is responsible when he attacks the security or welfare of the government, or the safety, character, and property of the individual.[45]

The second fundamental flaw in relying on the Pentagon Papers case is that the Court's *per curiam* opinion described a prior restraint on speech as "bearing a heavy presumption against its constitutional validity," but it was not an irrebuttable presumption for a majority of the Court. The classified information at issue in the case did not involve ongoing tactical intelligence-gathering operations such as those disclosed by the New York Times, and all but the most absolutist of First Amendment justices[46] and scholars have recognized, quite rightly, that the freedom of the press does not extend to publication of such things as troop movements. Justice White, for example, joined by Justice Stewart, expressly noted that he was not contending "that in no circumstances would the First Amendment permit an injunction against publishing information about government plans or operations," only that the government had not met "the very heavy burden that it must meet to warrant an injunction against publication."[47] Chief Justice Burger noted in his dissenting opinion that there are exceptions to the First Amendment, and that "[c]onceivably such exceptions may be lurking in these cases and would have been flushed had they been properly considered in the trial courts, free from unwarranted deadlines and frenetic pressures."[48] Justice Harlan, joined by the Chief Justice and Justice Blackmun, specifically wished to consider whether an injunction was appropriate in light of the "presumption" and "strong First Amendment policy" against prior restraints, thereby rejecting the absolutist view that would make his requested inquiry irrelevant.[49] And Justice Blackmun noted in his dissenting opinion that "even the newspapers concede that there are situations where restraint is in order and is constitutional."[50] In support of his position that the government has the right to prevent the publication of some sensitive information, albeit a "very narrow right," he cited no less a Justice than Oliver Wendell Holmes, whose own opinions on the First Amendment have charted the course of Supreme Court jurisprudence in the field for the better part of the past century. "It is a question of proximity and degree," noted Holmes in *Schenck v. United States*.[51] "When a nation is at war many things that might be said in time of peace are such a

---

[44] *Id.* at 755.

[45] Elliot's Debates, vol. 2, p. 449, *reprinted in* Neil H. Cogan, ed., The Complete Bill of rights: The Drafts, Debates, Sources, and Origins 99 (Oxford 1997).

[46] I refer here in particular to the concurring opinions of Justices Black, Douglas, and Brennan in *New York Times*, 403 U.S., at 714, 720, and 724.

[47] *Id.*, at 731.

[48] *Id.*, at 749.

[49] *Id.*, at 753, 754.

[50] *Id.*, at 761.

[51] 249 U.S. 47, 52 (1919).

hindrance to its effort that their utterance will not be endured so long as men fight and that no Court could regard them as protected by any constitutional right."[52]

In other words, the Pentagon Papers case comes with a very big caveat—one that is fully in line with prior precedent permitting prior restraints when the information at issue is highly sensitive classified information of ongoing military intelligence operations. In *Near v. Minnesota*, for example, the Supreme Court noted that "the protection even as to previous restraint is not unlimited," even though "the limitation has been recognized only in exceptional cases." Among the litany of exceptional cases mentioned by the Court was that "a government might prevent actual obstruction to its recruiting service or the publication of the sailing dates of transports or the number and location of troops."[53] Similarly, in *United States v. Reynolds*, the Court upheld the government's claim of privilege that investigation reports of an Air Force accident involving a plane that was testing classified electronics equipment need not be produced during discovery. Chief Justice Vinson, for the Court, offered this highly relevant explanation in support of the holding:

> In the instant case we cannot escape judicial notice that this is a time of vigorous preparation for national defense. Experience in the past was has made it common knowledge that air power is one of the most potent weapons in our scheme of defense, and that newly developing electronic devices have greatly enhanced the effective use of air power. *It is equally apparent that these electronic devices must be kept secret if their full military advantage is to be exploited in the national interests.* On the record before the trial court it appeared that this accident occurred to a military plane which had gone aloft to test secret electronic equipment. Certainly there was a reasonable danger that the accident investigation report would contain references to the secret electronic equipment which was the primary concern of the mission.[54]

It seems pretty clear that the disclosure of classified information about our intelligence-gathering capabilities and tactics fits within the "exceptional case" caveat recognized by a majority of the Court in both the Pentagon Papers case and in *Near*, and although the Supreme Court has never expressly held that such a caveat exists, neither has it held that the First Amendment bars the government from preventing the publication of classified information about ongoing, highly-sensitive military operations in the same way that it can prevent the dissemination of classified information by other citizens.

The second extraordinary claim made by Mr. Keller that needs to be addressed is the notion that the First Amendment's Freedom of the Press Clause creates a special preserve for the institutionalized press, as opposed to ordinary citizens. Although this is a common understanding among reporters and newspaper editors, it is wrong. The Freedom of the Press Clause was designed to protect the published word of all citizens, not just an institutionalized fourth estate. As one of the anti-federalist opponents of ratification of a constitution that did not include a bill of rights noted, the liberty of the press ensures that "the *people* have the right of expressing and publishing their sentiments upon every public measure."[55]

---

[52] *Id.*

[53] 283 U.S. 697, 716 (1931).

[54] 345 U.S. 1, 10 (1953) (emphasis added).

[55] Centinel, No. 2 (Oct. 24, 1787), reprinted in Cogan, The Complete Bill of Rights, at 103 (emphasis added).

James Madison's initial proposal for the First Amendment clearly expressed this common understanding, guaranteeing the right of the people "to speak, to write, or to publish their sentiments."[56] Roger Sherman's own proposal a month later mirrored Madison's:

> The people have certain natural rights which are retained by them when they enter into society, Such are the rights . . . of Speaking, writing and publishing their Sentiments with decency and freedom . . . . Of these rights therefore they Shall not be deprived by the government of the united States."[57]

These formulations were drawn from the amendments proposed by several of the state ratifying conventions,[58] and lest there be any doubt that "freedom of the press" was synonymous with the right of the people generally to speak, write, and publish their sentiments, the Pennsylvania proponents of a Bill of Rights made that amply clear: "That the people have a right to the freedom of speech, of writing, and of publishing their sentiments, *therefore*, the freedom of the press shall not be restrained by any law of the United States."[59] What is protected is not just the right to use a printing press or to go into the newspaper business, but the right of every citizen to publish, to make and distribute copies of words and/or pictures communicating his or her sentiments to the public. The founders would never have accepted the view that the freedom of the press is limited to members of a particular industry called "the press" or "the media."[60]

The consequence of this original understanding, of course, is that the First Amendment does not afford any greater protection to "the press" than it does to ordinary citizens, nor exempt "the press" from "the basic and simple duties of every citizen" to report information regarding discovery or possession of stolen property or secret government documents—a duty which Chief Justice Burger correctly noted rests equally "on taxi drivers, Justices, and the New York Times."[61]

Indeed, in analogous areas of media law involving matters with much lower stakes than national security, the Court has repeatedly emphasized that the media has no special exemption from generally applicable laws. The Court's holding in *Associated Press v. United*

---

[56] Annals of Congress, June 8, 1789, reprinted in Philip B. Kurland and Ralph Lerner, eds., 5 The Founders' Constitution 128 (1987).

[57] Cogan, *supra* n. 12, at 83.

[58] See, e.g., proposal of the North Carolina ratifying convention (Aug. 1, 1788) ("That the people have a right to freedom of speech, and of writing and publishing their sentiments; that the freedom of the press is one of the greatest bulwarks of Liberty, and ought not to be violated); proposal of the Rhode Island ratifying convention (May 29, 1790) ("That the people have a right to freedom of speech and of writing and publishing their sentiments, that the freedom of the press is one of the greatest bulwarks of liberty, and ought not to be violated); proposal of the Virginia ratifying convention (June 27, 1788) ("That the people have a right to freedom of speech, and of writing and publishing their Sentiments; that the freedom of the press is one of the greatest bulwarks of liberty and ought not to be violated), all reprinted in Cogan, *supra*, at 93.

[59] Pennsylvania Packet (Dec. 18, 1787), reprinted in Cogan, *supra*, at 93 (emphasis added).

[60] *See generally,* Thomas G. West, "Free Speech in the American Founding and in Modern Liberalism," in Ellen Frankel Paul, et al., eds., *Freedom of Speech* 310-384 (Cambridge University Press 2004).

[61] *New York Times*, 403 U.S., at 751.

States, for example, devastates any claim that the "press" has "a peculiar constitutional sanctuary" from the law:

> [W]e are not unmindful of the argument that newspaper publishers charged with combining cooperatively to violate the Sherman Act are entitled to have a different and more favorable kind of trial procedure than all other persons covered by the Act. No language in the Sherman Act or the summary judgment statute lends support to the suggestion. There is no single element in our traditional insistence upon an equally fair trial for every person from which any such discriminatory trial practice could stem. For equal-not unequal-justice under law is the goal of our society. Our legal system has not established different measures of proof for the trial of cases in which equally intelligent and responsible defendants are charged with violating the same statutes. Member publishers of AP are engaged in business for profit exactly as are other business men who sell food, steel, aluminum, or anything else people need or want. . . . All are alike covered by the Sherman Act. The fact that the publisher handles news while others handle food does not, as we shall later point out, afford the publisher a peculiar constitutional sanctuary in which he can with impunity violate laws regulating his business practices.[62]

Justice Harlan made the same point for the Court plurality in *Curtis Publishing Co. v. Butts*: "The publisher of a newspaper has no special immunity from the application of general laws."[63] And in the post-Pentagon Papers case of *Branzburg v. Hayes*, the Supreme Court refused to recognize a reporter/informant privilege that would exempt reporters from the obligation shared by other citizens to testify before a grand jury, explicitly noting that "otherwise valid laws serving substantial public interests may be enforced against the press as against others, despite the possible burden that may be imposed."[64]

So where does that leave us with respect to the New York Times' contentions? Once it is clear that the "Freedom of the Press" acknowledged in the First Amendment does not create a special preserve for the institutional media, the full import of Bill Keller's claims come into view, and it is the old saw, long since disproved, that democratic governments are not permitted secrets, even in time of war. Our Constitution expressly recognizes the common-sense necessity of government secrets, for example, in the Article I requirement that each House of Congress shall publish a journal of its proceedings, "excepting such Parts as in their Judgment may require Secrecy."[65] The need for secrecy is even more urgent in the executive branch, and as Alexander Hamilton noted in Federalist 71 (discussed above), it is one of the key reasons the Constitution provides for unity in the executive office, establishing an "energetic" executive who can operate with "secrecy" and "despatch" when necessary to protect "the community against foreign attacks."[66]

This need for secrecy in the conduct of certain executive functions such as those under consideration today has repeatedly been recognized and approved by the courts as well. Writing for the Court in *United States*, for example, Justice Sutherland explained why the

---

[62] 326 U.S. 1, 7 (1945) (internal citation omitted).

[63] 388 U.S. 130, 150 (1967). *See also, e.g., Associated Press v. National Labor Relations Board*, 301 U.S. 103 (1937) (no press exemption from labor laws).

[64] 408 U.S. 665, 682 (1972).

[65] U.S. Const. Art. I, § 5, cl. 3.

[66] The Federalist, No. 70, at 424 (Clinton Rossiter, ed., 1961).

President's authority over foreign affairs was so great, noting that he "has his confidential sources of information. He has his agents in the form of diplomatic, consular and other officials. Secrecy in respect of information gathered by them may be highly necessary, and the premature disclosure of it productive of harmful results."[67] A similar view was expressed by Justice Jackson in *Chicago & Southern Air Lines, Inc. v. Waterman Steamship Corp.*: "The President, both as Commander-in-Chief and as the Nation's organ for foreign affairs, has available intelligence services whose reports are not and *ought not to be published to the world.*"[68]

The constitutionality of protecting intelligence gathering and other operational military secrets in time of war is therefore beyond dispute, and the institutional press is no more permitted to ignore the legal restrictions imposed by the Espionage Act on the publication and other dissemination of such classified information than are ordinary citizens. Neither is it exempt from prosecution for willful violations of that Act.

Justice Goldberg famously noted in *Kennedy v. Mendoza-Martinez* that our Constitution "is not a suicide pact,"[69] and the sentiment is particularly apropos for the issues we are facing today. The simple fact is that the asymmetric nature of the current war against international terrorist organizations makes intelligence gathering the central and most critical front in the war. Not only must the executive branch aggressively pursue every legal means of gathering intelligence at its disposal, it must be equally aggressive in protecting the classified methods that it is using in that effort if it is to succeed in preventing future attacks on our homeland and fellow citizens such as those we witnessed on that fateful day in September nearly five years ago. Every citizen, including—particularly including—those employed with major media organs has a responsibility to prevent ongoing operational secrets from falling into the hands of our enemies by complying with the law regarding classified information. It is one of those "basic and simple duties" of citizenship that rests equally "on taxi drivers, Justices, and the New York Times."[70] We may never know how great the damage to our national security the recent disclosures of classified, highly-sensitive intelligence-gathering information have caused, but with the seriousness of the threat to our lives and liberty posed by terrorist organizations such as Al Qaida, it is certainly the right, and may well be the duty, of the executive to prosecute those responsible for them.

---

[67] 299 U.S. 304, 320 (1936).

[68] 333 U.S. 103, 111 (1948) (emphasis added).

[69] 372 U.S. 144, 160 (1963).

[70] *New York Times*, 403 U.S., at 751.

Kareem Shora

National Executive Director
American-Arab Anti Discrimination Committee (ADC)

On behalf of the American-Arab Anti Discrimination Committee (ADC), I wish to thank the U.S. Commission on Civil Rights for the opportunity to participate in today's briefing.

As the information made available today explains, ADC is the largest grassroots organization in the United States dedicated to protecting the civil rights and liberties of Arab Americans. ADC was established in 1980 by former US Senator James Abourezk and has grown into a national organization with headquarters in Washington, DC, fully-staffed regional offices in Massachusetts, New York, New Jersey, Michigan, and California, as well as 38 volunteer-based active chapters throughout the United States. My remarks today will follow the theme of this briefing, "Wiretapping in the War on Terror."

As part of that, I plan on highlighting some of the challenges encountered by the Arab, Muslim, and South Asian American communities as a result of this warrantless spying program and within the context of some US Government counter-terrorism measures stemming from the September 11, 2001, terrorist attacks on our nation.

The unfortunate, ineffective, and cosmetic actions undertaken by the US Government in the days, weeks, and months following the horrific September 11, 2001, terrorist attacks on our nation left a bitter taste within the Arab, Muslim, and South Asian American communities and a mark of shame on the fabric of our American society. To be just, in the past two years the Government has undertaken constructive proactive steps at regular dialogue with ADC and the Arab, Muslim, and South Asian American communities. This constructive approach has indeed resulted in addressing some very serious rights violations in what can only be categorized as a professional and, on average, consistent manner. We as Arab Americans publicly acknowledge and thank our government for doing so.

Moreover, since the horrific September 11, 2001 terrorist attacks, Arab Americans have recognized the special role they have as partners with law enforcement and other government agencies in protecting our country. ADC and others can provide multiple examples where we stood shoulder-to-shoulder with law enforcement agencies, providing our resources and coordinating efforts to complement the US Government's legitimate efforts in combating terrorism and violent extremism. A specific example of such coordination includes the ADC Diversity and Law Enforcement Outreach Program that we launched in 2002. This program has trained approximately eight-thousand of our law enforcement officials in cultural competency; providing them with the necessary tools to exercise their duties more efficiently and effectively by expertly differentiating actual threats and behavior from cultural or religious norms and mores associated with Arab culture and Islam, in addition to providing specific community partners available to coordinate legitimate efforts with federal law enforcement around the nation. However, and with that said, many challenges remain unresolved including those associated with both the substance and perception of warrantless domestic spying.

Many of the so-called counter-terrorism programs initiated by the US Government in 2001 and 2002 directly targeted our communities based on national origin. These were programs such as the now infamous and ineffective National Security Entry-Exit Registration System (NSEERS), commonly known as the "Special Registration Program," the FBI "voluntary interview" initiatives, and the challenges associated with the multiple "watch" and "no fly" lists. In its public defense of these programs, the US Government is yet to point to a single terrorist charged with terrorism as a result of these targeted programs. Indeed, the only impact of which we are aware is disproportionate enforcement that continues to place the spotlight of suspicion on the Arab, Muslim, and South Asian American populations.

Four years ago, President Bush ordered the National Security Agency (NSA) to illegally spy on American citizens by monitoring electronic communication, including phone conversations, made between the United States and foreign countries. Later information and Congressional testimonies have made clear that it was, or is, communication between the United States and countries in the Middle East that were, or are, in the crosshairs of this program. While the national security of the United States should be at the forefront of government efforts, we should make sure that those efforts are efficient, effective, and not self-defeating gestures that cost us billions of dollars in taxpayer money while at the same time clogging up our intelligence and law enforcement agencies with a traffic jam of data awaiting translation and processing.

In authorizing this warrantless spying program, President Bush violated the law and trampled on our most fundamental liberties. However, and my focus here today, is in the damage this has caused as a result of the apprehension it has created within the Arab American community and the echoing negative effects that continue to reverberate in the Middle East today.

As we all know, following the authorization of the spying program, President Bush launched a public diplomacy campaign to "win the hearts and minds" of people in the Middle East. However, the program, both under its previous iteration under the NSA as well as under its current form, has killed any chances of success for this campaign at winning any hearts or minds of people in the Middle East. Arab Americans and others representing the Muslim and South Asian population with family ties to that part of the world are now afraid of communicating with their family members by phone because of the uncertainty of whether the conversations, often in Arabic or other Middle Eastern or South Asian languages, will be misunderstood or mistranslated by the NSA.

It was indeed a shame to see President Bush publicly and repeatedly defending this program. It is most shameful to learn that American citizens now presume that their phone conversations with their family members in the old country are being recorded by government agencies with few precious resources and fewer qualified professionals able to process the information being recorded. The American people need to ask how we can allegedly promote democracy in the Middle East when our President has elected to trample upon it at home.

This program cannot be analyzed in isolation and must be viewed in light of what we publicly know has taken place as part of the Government's efforts in the War on Terror during the past few years. As I indicated earlier, another program adopted by the US Government under the umbrella of counter terrorism was the FBI's "voluntary interview" initiatives. These interviews, which were initiated in 2001 and 2002 but which continue to take place today on a more informal basis, demonstrated that individual Constitutional liberties and protections were being used by the FBI in its threat-assessment processes. Specifically, examples collected by ADC have demonstrated that some FBI agents and other law enforcement officials who engage in these interviews as part of the multiple Joint Terrorism Task Forces violate their publicly-stated parameters and engage in "Patriotism tests" of some individuals. While the manner by which the FBI obtains its information is classified, and understandably must remain so, questions such as individual religious practice, political views about the war in Iraq and the Palestinian-Israeli conflict, and religious affiliation and practice (including some inquiries of whether a person is a Sunni or Shiia Muslim and how many times per week a person elects to pray) continue to be asked. These examples, although rare in frequency, have increased the negative perceptions of the US Government, and specifically the FBI and law enforcement, within the Arab, Muslim, and South Asian American communities and have caused many to question whether there is a link between the FBI's domestic investigative efforts and the warrantless spying program.

Moreover, the US Government is yet to effectively address the name confusion and misidentification of individuals whose names might be similar to ones located on one of the Government's "watch" or "no fly" lists. Anecdotal examples suggest that Arab, Muslim, and South Asian Americans are more likely to be flagged by Department of Homeland Security authorities either when traveling by air domestically or when returning from international travel to a United States land or airport. This includes visitors, as well as immigrants, permanent residents, and, most importantly, US citizens. Although the US Government's position states that it does not profile individuals based on race, ethnicity, or religion, the "watch" and "no fly" list challenges have created a tremendous level of mistrust and the perception of ethnic and racial profiling on the part of the Arab, Muslim, and South Asian American populations in the United States. While it is impossible to obtain proof of specific links between the "watch" and "no fly" lists and the warrantless spying program, it is a legitimate assumption that these initiatives might be related and that information collected under that program may easily be fed into these lists regardless of whether the information was appropriately analyzed by qualified experts or not.

Due to the secret nature of the warrantless spying program, we cannot provide specific examples unequivocally demonstrating the negative effects it has had on the Arab, Muslim, and South Asian American communities' rights. However, anecdotal examples suggest such effects. One example was documented by ADC in 2004 when Dr. Z, an American citizen of Arab origin, received a phone call from an FBI Special Agent. While extremely professional and courteous, the FBI agent requested to meet Dr. Z for a casual chat about telephone calls made from the Dr. Z's home phone number in recent weeks. Dr. Z contacted ADC which provided an attorney to monitor the meeting. Our attorney documented that the FBI agent, despite his professionalism and courtesy during the meeting, questioned Dr. Z for having regular phone calls made to a specific city in an Arab country on a regular basis over a period of two months. Dr. Z explained during this meeting that his mother-in-law was ill at the time and thus his wife was away visiting her. Therefore, Dr. Z was making phone calls to that specific city on a regular basis to speak with his wife as she visited her ill mother. To verify, the FBI agent produced a copy of call-logs made from Dr. Z's home telephone number to a specific area in that city; an Arab capital. When asked by the ADC attorney whether the FBI is monitoring Dr. Z's telephone and whether they have any warrants to do so, the agent stated that the FBI was not monitoring Dr. Z's phone number and that if they were they would have to alert Dr. Z of such monitoring and provide a copy of the warrant upon speaking with him about the information they collected through such monitoring. The FBI agent additionally indicated that the information presented in the call-log was provided through "intelligence" sources and not through any domestic FBI efforts. He indicated that the FBI was simply following-up on a request provided through those "intelligence" sources.

It should be noted, and I am here on record to document, that the perceived injustice, whether correct or incorrect, of singling out people based on national origin (and ultimately religion) and, in turn, penalizing them for exercising their First Amendment rights within our nation may have significantly harmed the relationship of trust between law enforcement and the Arab, Muslim, and South Asian American communities—a relationship that is vital to the national security of the United States and the safety of those communities. The ill effects of this program, be it as it stood within the National Security Agency, or in its current form under the supervision of the Foreign Intelligence Surveillance Court, continue to reverberate and exacerbate the negative perception of the United States in the Middle East, thus, adding hostility and apprehension in a region of the world where we most need friends and allies.

In summary, US Government agencies have taken many proactive steps at constructive dialogue and communication in the past few years. However, the unfortunate actions the US Government undertook in the days, weeks, and months following the September 11, 2001, terrorist attacks continue to reverberate their negative and destructive effects on the Arab, Muslim, and South Asian American communities and in turn on our entire nation today. Compiled with the more substantive challenges such as the National Security Entry-Exit Registration System (NSEERS), the FBI's so-called "voluntary interviews," and the problems associated with the "watch" and "no fly" lists, the warrantless spying program is yet another miscalculation made by our government that only serve to hurt the national security of our nation.

Today we as Arab Americans both publicly thank the US Government for the proactive steps it has taken to fix the mistakes it created after 9/11 while at the same time call upon its leaders and upon the US Congress to do more to protect our nation by improving our image abroad; especially in parts of the world where we need more allies and friends.

The lesson we have learned as a people is not to strip the most valuable treasure we have as a nation by ignoring the basic rights and liberties and inherently weakening the great American values of freedom, fairness, and equality we have championed for decades. Let us not compromise our values as we attempt to reach a compromise that secures our nation while keeping our hearts and minds open wide. Thank you.

Speaker Biographies

Gregory Nojeim

Gregory T. Nojeim is the Associate Director and Chief Legislative Counsel of the American Civil Liberties Union's Washington Legislative Office. The ACLU is a non-partisan organization with hundreds of thousands of activists and members and 53 affiliates nation-wide devoted to protecting the principles of freedom and equality set forth in the U.S. Constitution and civil rights laws. In this capacity, he coordinates the ACLU's legislative strategies, supervises its lobbyists and policy counsels, and helps to develop the ACLU position and message on pending legislation. He helped spearhead the ACLU's response to the September 11, 2001 terrorist attacks.

Mr. Nojeim started at the ACLU in 1995, and has been responsible for analyzing the civil liberties implications of federal legislation relating to terrorism, national security, immigration, and informational privacy. He frequently testifies before congressional committees and the various commissions Congress establishes.

Prior to assuming his position with the ACLU, Mr. Nojeim was for four years the Director of Legal Services of the American-Arab Anti Discrimination Committee (ADC). He conducted much of ADC's work in the immigration, civil rights, and human rights areas. Mr. Nojeim was employed for five years as an attorney with the Washington, DC law firm of Kirkpatrick & Lockhart, where he specialized in mergers and acquisitions, securities law, and international trade. He graduated *magna cum laude* from the University of Rochester in 1981, where he studied political science. He received his J.D. degree from the University of Virginia in 1985, and sat on the editorial board of the *Virginia Journal of International Law*.

John Eastman

Dr. John Eastman, Interim Associate Dean of Administration, Henry Salvatori Professor of Law & Community Service, joined the faculty of the Chapman University School of Law in August 1999, specializing in Constitutional Law, Legal History, Civil Procedure, and Property. He is also the Director of the Center for Constitutional Jurisprudence, a public interest law firm affiliated with the Claremont Institute for the Study of Statesmanship and Political Philosophy. He has a Ph.D. in Government from the Claremont Graduate School and a J.D. degree from the University of Chicago Law School.

Prior to joining the Chapman law faculty, Dr. Eastman served as a law clerk to the Honorable Clarence Thomas, Associate Justice, Supreme Court of the United States, and to the Honorable J. Michael Luttig, Judge, United States Court of Appeals for the Fourth Circuit. He practiced law with the national law firm of Kirkland & Ellis, representing major corporate clients in federal and state courts and with respect to state attorneys general investigations, in complex commercial contract litigation and in consumer litigation.

Dr. Eastman has appeared as an expert legal commentator on numerous television and radio programs, testified before the U.S. Congress, and published numerous op-eds in newspapers around the country.

Kareem Shora

Kareem W. Shora, JD, LLM is National Executive Director at the American-Arab Anti Discrimination Committee (ADC). Shora, who joined ADC in 2000 as legal advisor, has served most recently as Legal Department and Policy Director with ADC before being named to this position in early 2007.

Shora has been published by the *National Law Journal*; *TRIAL Magazine*; the Georgetown University Law Center's *Journal on Poverty Law and Public Policy*; the Harvard University JFK School of Government *Asian American Policy Review*; the American Bar Association (ABA) *Air and Space Lawyer*; and the Yeshiva University Cardozo Public Law, *Policy and Ethics Journal*. He is also a professor of Foreign Policy at the American University Washington Semester Program.

Shora was a featured speaker on three panels during the 2002 American Bar Association (ABA) National Meeting in Washington, DC, testified during the United Nations Commission on Human Rights 59th Annual Meeting in Geneva, Switzerland, in April, 2003, participated as a speaker during the 2005 Organization for Security and Cooperation in Europe (OSCE) conference on Anti-Semitism and Other Forms of Intolerance in Cordoba, Spain, the 2005 OSCE Human Dimensions Implementation Meeting in Warsaw, Poland, and the OSCE 2006 conference on anti-Muslim Intolerance in Warsaw. He most recently testified at the G8 Experts Roundtable on Diversity and Integration in Lisbon, Portugal. He has spoken about civil rights, civil liberties and immigration policy with many national and international media outlets.

Shora, who was born in Damascus, Syria, holds a Doctor of Jurisprudence (JD) degree from West Virginia University (WVU) College of Law and the LL.M. specialty in International Legal Studies from American University Washington College of Law.

Appendix A

Attachment to Statement of Gregory Nojeim

January 9, 2006

The Hon. Bill Frist, Majority Leader
United States Senate
Washington, DC 20510

The Hon. J. Dennis Hastert, Speaker
U.S. House of Representatives
Washington, DC 20515

The Hon. Arlen Specter, Chairman
Senate Judiciary Committee
United States Senate
Washington, DC 20510

The Hon. F. James Sensenbrenner, Jr.
Chairman
House Judiciary Committee
U.S. House of Representatives
Washington, DC 20515

The Hon. Pat Roberts
Chairman
Senate Select Committee on Intelligence
United States Senate
Washington, DC 20510

The Hon. Peter Hoekstra
Chairman
Permanent Select Committee
on Intelligence
U.S. House of Representatives
Washington, DC 20515

The Hon. Harry Reid, Minority Leader
United States Senate
Washington, DC 20510

The Hon. Nancy Pelosi, Minority Leader
U.S. House of Representatives
Washington, DC 20515

The Hon. Patrick Leahy, Ranking Minority
Member–Senate Judiciary Committee
United States Senate
Washington, D.C. 20510

The Hon. John Conyers
Ranking Minority Member
House Judiciary Committee
U.S. House of Representatives
Washington, DC 20515

The Hon. John D. Rockefeller, IV
Vice Chairman
Senate Select Committee on Intelligence
United States Senate
Washington, DC 20510

The Hon. Jane Harman
Ranking Minority Member
Permanent Select Committee
on Intelligence
U.S. House of Representatives
Washington, DC 20515

Dear Members of Congress:

We are scholars of constitutional law and former government officials. We write in our individual capacities as citizens concerned by the Bush Administration's National Security Agency domestic spying program, as reported in the New York Times, and in particular to respond to the Justice Department's December 22, 2005 letter to the majority and minority leaders of the House and Senate Intelligence Committees setting forth the administration's defense of the program.[1] Although the program's secrecy prevents us from being privy to all of its details, the Justice Department's defense of what it concedes was secret and warrantless electronic surveillance of persons within the United States fails to identify any plausible legal authority for such surveillance. Accordingly the program appears on its face to violate existing law.

The basic legal question here is not new. In 1978, after an extensive investigation of the privacy violations associated with foreign intelligence surveillance programs, Congress and the President enacted the Foreign Intelligence Surveillance Act (FISA). Pub. L. 95-511, 92 Stat. 1783. FISA comprehensively regulates electronic surveillance within the United States, striking a careful balance between protecting civil liberties and preserving the "vitally important government purpose" of obtaining valuable intelligence in order to safeguard national security. S. Rep. No. 95-604, pt. 1, at 9 (1977).

With minor exceptions, FISA authorizes electronic surveillance only upon certain specified showings, and only if approved by a court. The statute specifically allows for warrantless *wartime* domestic electronic surveillance—but only for the first fifteen days of a war. 50 U.S.C. § 1811. It makes criminal any electronic surveillance not authorized by statute, *id.* §1809; and it expressly establishes FISA and specified provisions of the federal criminal code (which govern wiretaps for criminal investigation) as the "*exclusive* means by which electronic surveillance…may be conducted," 18 U.S.C. § 2511(2)(f) (emphasis added).[2]

The Department of Justice concedes that the NSA program was not authorized by any of the above provisions. It maintains, however, that the program did not violate existing law because Congress implicitly authorized the NSA program when it enacted the Authorization for Use of Military Force (AUMF) against al Qaeda, Pub. L. No. 107-40, 115 Stat. 224 (2001). But the AUMF cannot reasonably be construed to implicitly authorize warrantless electronic surveillance in the United States during wartime, where Congress has expressly and specifically addressed that precise question in FISA and limited any such warrantless surveillance to the first fifteen days of war.

---

[1] The Justice Department letter can be found at www.nationalreview.com/pdf/12%2022%2005%20NSA%20letter.pdf.

[2] More detail about the operation of FISA can be found in Congressional Research Service, "Presidential Authority to Conduct Warrantless Electronic Surveillance to Gather Foreign Intelligence Information" (Jan. 5, 2006). This letter was drafted prior to release of the CRS Report, which corroborates the conclusions drawn here.

The DOJ also invokes the President's inherent constitutional authority as Commander in Chief to collect "signals intelligence" targeted at the enemy, and maintains that construing FISA to prohibit the President's actions would raise constitutional questions. But even conceding that the President in his role as Commander in Chief may generally collect signals intelligence on the enemy abroad, Congress indisputably has authority to regulate electronic surveillance within the United States, as it has done in FISA. Where Congress has so regulated, the President can act in contravention of statute only if his authority is *exclusive*, and not subject to the check of statutory regulation. The DOJ letter pointedly does not make that extraordinary claim.

Moreover, to construe the AUMF as the DOJ suggests would itself raise serious constitutional questions under the Fourth Amendment. The Supreme Court has never upheld warrantless wiretapping within the United States. Accordingly, the principle that statutes should be construed to avoid serious constitutional questions provides an additional reason for concluding that the AUMF does not authorize the President's actions here.

I. CONGRESS DID NOT IMPLICITLY AUTHORIZE THE NSA DOMESTIC SPYING PROGRAM IN THE AUMF, AND IN FACT EXPRESSLY PROHIBITED IT IN FISA

The DOJ concedes (Letter at 4) that the NSA program involves "electronic surveillance," which is defined in FISA to mean the interception of the *contents* of telephone, wire, or email communications that occur, at least in part, in the United States. 50 U.S.C. §§ 1801(f)(1)-(2), 1801(n). NSA engages in such surveillance without judicial approval, and apparently without the substantive showings that FISA requires—e.g., that the subject is an "agent of a foreign power." *Id.* § 1805(a). The DOJ does not argue that FISA itself authorizes such electronic surveillance; and, as the DOJ letter acknowledges, 18 U.S.C. § 1809 makes criminal any electronic surveillance not authorized by statute.

The DOJ nevertheless contends that the surveillance is authorized by the AUMF, signed on September 18, 2001, which empowers the President to use "all necessary and appropriate force against" al Qaeda. According to the DOJ, collecting "signals intelligence" on the enemy, even if it involves tapping U.S. phones without court approval or probable cause, is a "fundamental incident of war" authorized by the AUMF. This argument fails for four reasons.

First, and most importantly, the DOJ's argument rests on an unstated general "implication" from the AUMF that directly contradicts *express* and *specific* language in FISA. Specific and "carefully drawn" statutes prevail over general statutes where there is a conflict. *Morales v. TWA, Inc.*, 504 U.S. 374, 384-85 (1992) (quoting *International Paper Co. v. Ouelette*, 479 U.S. 481, 494 (1987)). In FISA, Congress has directly and specifically spoken on the question of domestic warrantless wiretapping, including during wartime, and it could not have spoken more clearly.

As noted above, Congress has comprehensively regulated all electronic surveillance in the United States, and authorizes such surveillance only pursuant to specific statutes designated as the "*exclusive* means by which electronic surveillance…and the interception of domestic wire, oral, and electronic communications may be conducted." 18 U.S.C. § 2511(2)(f) (emphasis added). Moreover, FISA *specifically* addresses the question of domestic wiretapping during wartime. In a provision entitled "Authorization during time of war," FISA dictates that "[n]otwithstanding any other law, the President, through the Attorney General, may authorize electronic surveillance without a court order under this subchapter to acquire foreign intelligence information *for a period not to exceed fifteen calendar days following a declaration of war by the Congress.*" 50 U.S.C. § 1811 (emphasis added). Thus, even where Congress has declared war—a more formal step than an authorization such as the AUMF—the law limits warrantless wiretapping to the first fifteen days of the conflict. Congress explained that if the President needed further warrantless surveillance during wartime, the fifteen days would be sufficient for Congress to consider and enact further authorization.[3] Rather than follow this course, the President acted unilaterally and secretly in contravention of FISA's terms. The DOJ letter remarkably does not even *mention* FISA's fifteen-day war provision, which directly refutes the President's asserted "implied" authority.

In light of the specific and comprehensive regulation of FISA, especially the fifteen-day war provision, there is no basis for finding in the AUMF's general language implicit authority for unchecked warrantless domestic wiretapping. As Justice Frankfurter stated in rejecting a similar argument by President Truman when he sought to defend the seizure of the steel mills during the Korean War on the basis of implied congressional authorization:

> It is one thing to draw an intention of Congress from general language and to say that Congress would have explicitly written what is inferred, where Congress has not addressed itself to a specific situation. It is quite impossible, however, when Congress did specifically address itself to a problem, as Congress did to that of seizure, to find secreted in the interstices of legislation the very grant of power which Congress consciously withheld. To find authority so explicitly withheld is … to disrespect the whole legislative process and the constitutional division of authority between President and Congress.

Youngstown Sheet & Tube Co. v. Sawyer, 343 U.S. 579, 609 (1952) (Frankfurter, J., concurring).

Second, the DOJ's argument would require the conclusion that Congress implicitly and *sub silentio* repealed 18 U.S.C. § 2511(2)(f), the provision that identifies FISA and specific criminal code provisions as "the *exclusive* means by which electronic surveillance…may be conducted." Repeals by implication are strongly disfavored; they can be established only by "overwhelming evidence," *J.E.M. Ag. Supply, Inc. v. Pioneer Hi-Bred Int'l, Inc.*, 534 U.S. 124, 137 (2001), and "'the only permissible justification for a repeal by implication is when the earlier and later statutes are irreconcilable,'" *id.* at 141-142 (quoting *Morton v. Mancari*, 417 U.S. 535, 550 (1974)). The AUMF and § 2511(2)(f) are not

---

[3] "The Conferees intend that this [15-day] period will allow time for consideration of any amendment to this act that may be appropriate during a wartime emergency. . . . The conferees expect that such amendment would be reported with recommendations within 7 days and that each House would vote on the amendment within 7 days thereafter." H.R. Conf. Rep. No. 95-1720, at 34 (1978).

irreconcilable, and there is *no* evidence, let alone overwhelming evidence, that Congress intended to repeal § 2511(2)(f).

Third, Attorney General Alberto Gonzales has admitted that the administration did not seek to amend FISA to authorize the NSA spying program because it was advised that Congress would reject such an amendment.[4] The administration cannot argue on the one hand that Congress authorized the NSA program in the AUMF, and at the same time that it did not ask Congress for such authorization because it feared Congress would say no.[5]

Finally, the DOJ's reliance upon *Hamdi v. Rumsfeld*, 542 U.S. 507 (2004), to support its reading of the AUMF, *see* DOJ Letter at 3, is misplaced. A plurality of the Court in *Hamdi* held that the AUMF authorized military detention of enemy combatants captured on the battlefield abroad as a "fundamental incident of waging war." *Id.* at 519. The plurality expressly limited this holding to individuals who were "part of or supporting forces hostile to the United States or coalition partners *in Afghanistan and who engaged in an armed conflict against the United States there.*" *Id.* at 516 (emphasis added). It is one thing, however, to say that foreign battlefield capture of enemy combatants is an incident of waging war that Congress intended to authorize. It is another matter entirely to treat unchecked warrantless *domestic* spying as included in that authorization, especially where an existing statute specifies that other laws are the "exclusive means" by which electronic surveillance may be conducted and provides that even a declaration of war authorizes such spying only for a fifteen-day emergency period.[6]

---

[4] Attorney General Gonzales stated, "We have had discussions with Congress in the past—certain members of Congress—as to whether or not FISA could be amended to allow us to adequately deal with this kind of threat, and we were advised that that would be difficult, if not impossible." Press Briefing by Attorney General Alberto Gonzales and General Michael Hayden, Principal Deputy Director for National Intelligence (Dec. 19, 2005), *available at* http://www.whitehouse.gov/news/releases/2005/12/20051219-1.html.

[5] The administration had a convenient vehicle for seeking any such amendment in the USA PATRIOT Act of 2001, Pub. L. No. 107-56, 115 Stat. 272, enacted in October 2001. The Patriot Act amended FISA in several respects, including in sections 218 (allowing FISA wiretaps in criminal investigations) and 215 (popularly known as the "libraries provision"). Yet the administration did not ask Congress to amend FISA to authorize the warrantless electronic surveillance at issue here.

[6] The DOJ attempts to draw an analogy between FISA and 18 U.S.C. § 4001(a), which provides that the United States may not detain a U.S. citizen "except pursuant to an act of Congress." The DOJ argues that just as the AUMF was deemed to authorize the detention of Hamdi, 542 U.S. at 519, so the AUMF satisfies FISA's requirement that electronic surveillance be "authorized by statute." DOJ Letter at 3-4. The analogy is inapt. As noted above, FISA specifically limits warrantless domestic wartime surveillance to the first fifteen days of the conflict, and 18 U.S.C. § 2511(2)(f) specifies that existing law is the "exclusive means" for domestic wiretapping. Section 4001(a), by contrast, neither expressly addresses detention of the enemy during wartime nor attempts to create an exclusive mechanism for detention. Moreover, the analogy overlooks the carefully limited holding and rationale of the *Hamdi* plurality, which found the AUMF to be an "explicit congressional authorization for the detention of individuals in the narrow category we describe . . . . who fought against the United States in Afghanistan as part of the Taliban, an organization known to have supported the al Qaeda terrorist network," and whom "Congress sought to target in passing the AUMF" 542 U.S. at 518. By the government's own admission, the NSA program is by no means so limited. *See* Gonzales/Hayden Press Briefing, *supra* note 4.

II. CONSTRUING FISA TO PROHIBIT WARRANTLESS DOMESTIC WIRETAPPING DOES NOT RAISE ANY SERIOUS CONSTITUTIONAL QUESTION, WHEREAS CONSTRUING THE AUMF TO AUTHORIZE SUCH WIRETAPPING WOULD RAISE SERIOUS QUESTIONS UNDER THE FOURTH AMENDMENT

The DOJ argues that FISA and the AUMF should be construed to permit the NSA program's domestic surveillance because otherwise there might be a "conflict between FISA and the President's Article II authority as Commander-in-Chief." DOJ Letter at 4. The statutory scheme described above is not ambiguous, and therefore the constitutional avoidance doctrine is not even implicated. *See United States v. Oakland Cannabis Buyers' Coop.*, 532 U.S. 483, 494 (2001) (the "canon of constitutional avoidance has no application in the absence of statutory ambiguity"). But were it implicated, it would work against the President, not in his favor. Construing FISA and the AUMF according to their plain meanings raises no serious constitutional questions regarding the President's duties under Article II. Construing the AUMF to *permit* unchecked warrantless wiretapping without probable cause, however, would raise serious questions under the Fourth Amendment.

A. FISA's Limitations Are Consistent with the President's Article II Role

We do not dispute that, absent congressional action, the President might have inherent constitutional authority to collect "signals intelligence" about the enemy abroad. Nor do we dispute that, had Congress taken no action in this area, the President might well be constitutionally empowered to conduct domestic surveillance directly tied and narrowly confined to that goal—subject, of course, to Fourth Amendment limits. Indeed, in the years before FISA was enacted, the federal law involving wiretapping specifically provided that "[n]othing contained in this chapter or in section 605 of the Communications Act of 1934 shall limit the constitutional power of the President...to obtain foreign intelligence information deemed essential to the security of the United States." 18 U.S.C. § 2511(3) (1976).

But FISA specifically *repealed* that provision. FISA § 201(c), 92 Stat. 1797, and replaced it with language dictating that FISA and the criminal code are the "exclusive means" of conducting electronic surveillance. In doing so, Congress did not deny that the President has constitutional power to conduct electronic surveillance for national security purposes; rather, Congress properly concluded that "even if the President has the inherent authority *in the absence of legislation* to authorize warrantless electronic surveillance for foreign intelligence purposes, Congress has the power to regulate the conduct of such surveillance by legislating a reasonable procedure, which then becomes the exclusive means by which such surveillance may be conducted." H.R. Rep. No. 95-1283, pt. 1, at 24 (1978) (emphasis added). This analysis, Congress noted, was "supported by two successive Attorneys General." *Id.*

To say that the President has inherent authority does not mean that his authority is exclusive, or that his conduct is not subject to statutory regulations enacted (as FISA was) pursuant to Congress's Article I powers. As Justice Jackson famously explained in his influential opinion in *Youngstown Sheet & Tube Co. v. Sawyer*, 343 U.S. at 635 (Jackson, J., concurring), the Constitution "enjoins upon its branches separateness but interdependence, autonomy but reciprocity. Presidential powers are not fixed but fluctuate, depending upon their disjunction or conjunction with those of Congress." For example, the President in his role as Commander in Chief directs military operations. But the Framers gave Congress the power to prescribe rules for the regulation of the armed and naval forces, Art. I, § 8, cl. 14, and if a duly enacted statute prohibits the military from engaging in torture or cruel, inhuman, and degrading treatment, the President must follow that dictate. As Justice Jackson wrote, when the President acts in defiance of "the expressed or implied will of Congress," his power is "at its lowest ebb." 343 U.S. at 637. In this setting, Jackson wrote, "Presidential power [is] most vulnerable to attack and in the least favorable of possible constitutional postures." *Id.* at 640.

Congress plainly has authority to regulate domestic wiretapping by federal agencies under its Article I powers, and the DOJ does not suggest otherwise. Indeed, when FISA was enacted, the Justice Department agreed that Congress had power to regulate such conduct, and could require judicial approval of foreign intelligence surveillance.[7] FISA does not prohibit foreign intelligence surveillance, but merely imposes reasonable regulation to protect legitimate privacy rights. (For example, although FISA generally requires judicial approval for electronic surveillance of persons within the United States, it permits the executive branch to install a wiretap immediately so long as it obtains judicial approval within 72 hours. 50 U.S.C. § 1805(f).)

Just as the President is bound by the statutory prohibition on torture, he is bound by the statutory dictates of FISA.[8] The DOJ once infamously argued that the President as Commander in Chief could ignore even the criminal prohibition on torture,[9] and, more broadly still, that statutes may not "place *any* limits on the President's determinations as to any terrorist threat, the amount of military force to be used in response, or the method, timing, and nature of the response."[10] But the administration withdrew the August 2002 torture memo after it was disclosed, and for good reason the DOJ does not advance these

---

[7] *See, e.g.,* S. Rep. No. 95-604, pt. I, at 16 (1977) (Congress's assertion of power to regulate the President's authorization of electronic surveillance for foreign intelligence purposes was "concurred in by the Attorney General"); Foreign Intelligence Electronic Surveillance: Hearings Before the Subcomm. on Legislation of the House Permanent Select Comm. on Intelligence, 95th Cong., 2d Sess., at 31 (1978) (Letter from John M. Harmon, Assistant Attorney General, Office of Legal Counsel, to Edward P. Boland, Chairman, House Permanent Select Comm. on Intelligence (Apr. 18, 1978)) ("it seems unreasonable to conclude that Congress, in the exercise of its powers in this area, may not vest in the courts the authority to approve intelligence surveillance").

[8] Indeed, Article II imposes on the President the general *obligation* to enforce laws that Congress has validly enacted, including FISA: "he *shall* take Care that the Laws be faithfully executed." (emphasis added). The use of the mandatory "shall" indicates that under our system of separated powers, he is duty-bound to execute the provisions of FISA, not defy them.

[9] *See* Memorandum from Jay S. Bybee, Assistant Attorney General, Department of Justice Office of Legal Counsel, to Alberto R. Gonzales, Counsel to the President, Re: *Standards of Conduct for Interrogation under 18 U.S.C. §§ 2340-2340A* (Aug. 1, 2002), at 31.

[10] Memorandum from John C. Yoo, Deputy Assistant Attorney General, Office of Legal Counsel, to the Deputy Counsel to the President, Re: *The President's Constitutional Authority To Conduct Military Operations Against Terrorists And Nations Supporting Them* (Sept. 25, 2001), *available at* www.usdoj.gov/olc/warpowers925.htm (emphasis added).

extreme arguments here. Absent a serious question about FISA's constitutionality, there is no reason even to consider construing the AUMF to have implicitly overturned the carefully designed regulatory regime that FISA establishes. *See, e.g., Reno v. Flores*, 507 U.S. 292, 314 n.9 (1993) (constitutional avoidance canon applicable only if the constitutional question to be avoided is a serious one, "not to eliminate all possible contentions that the statute *might* be unconstitutional") (emphasis in original; citation omitted).[11]

B. Construing the AUMF to Authorize Warrantless Domestic Wiretapping Would Raise Serious Constitutional Questions

The principle that ambiguous statutes should be construed to avoid serious constitutional questions works against the administration, not in its favor. Interpreting the AUMF and FISA to permit unchecked domestic wiretapping for the duration of the conflict with al Qaeda would certainly raise serious constitutional questions. The Supreme Court has never upheld such a sweeping power to invade the privacy of Americans at home without individualized suspicion or judicial oversight.

The NSA surveillance program permits wiretapping within the United States without *either* of the safeguards presumptively required by the Fourth Amendment for electronic surveillance—individualized probable cause and a warrant or other order issued by a judge or magistrate. The Court has long held that wiretaps generally require a warrant and probable cause. *Katz v. United States*, 389 U.S. 347 (1967). And the only time the Court considered the question of national security wiretaps, it held that the Fourth Amendment prohibits domestic security wiretaps without those safeguards. *United States v. United States Dist. Court*, 407 U.S. 297 (1972). Although the Court in that case left open the question of the Fourth Amendment validity of warrantless wiretaps for foreign intelligence purposes, its precedents raise serious constitutional questions about the kind of open-ended authority the President has asserted with respect to the NSA program. *See id.* at 316-18 (explaining difficulty of guaranteeing Fourth Amendment freedoms if domestic surveillance can be conducted solely in the discretion of the executive branch).

Indeed, serious Fourth Amendment questions about the validity of warrantless wiretapping led Congress to enact FISA, in order to "provide the secure framework by which the executive branch may conduct legitimate electronic surveillance for foreign intelligence purposes within the context of this nation's commitment to privacy and individual rights." S. Rep. No. 95- 604, pt. 1, at 15 (1977) (citing, *inter alia, Zweibon v. Mitchell*, 516 F.2d 594 (D.C. Cir. 1975), in which "the court of appeals held that a warrant must be obtained before a

---

[11] Three years ago, the FISA Court of Review suggested in dictum that Congress cannot "encroach on the President's constitutional power" to conduct foreign intelligence surveillance. *In re Sealed Case No. 02-001*, 310 F.3d 717, 742 (FIS Ct. Rev. 2002) (*per curiam*). The FISA Court of Review, however, did not hold that FISA was unconstitutional, nor has any other court suggested that FISA's modest regulations constitute an impermissible encroachment on presidential authority. The FISA Court of Review relied upon *United States v. Truong Dihn Hung*, 629 F.2d 908 (4th Cir. 1980)—but that court did not suggest that the President's powers were beyond congressional control. To the contrary, the *Truong* court indicated that FISA's restrictions *were* constitutional. *See* 629 F.2d at 915 n.4 (noting that "the imposition of a warrant requirement, beyond the constitutional minimum described in this opinion, *should be left to the intricate balancing performed in the course of the legislative process by Congress and the President*") (emphasis added).

wiretap is installed on a domestic organization that is neither the agent of, nor acting in collaboration with, a foreign power").

Relying on *In re Sealed Case No. 02-001*, the DOJ argues that the NSA program falls within an exception to the warrant and probable cause requirement for reasonable searches that serve "special needs" above and beyond ordinary law enforcement. But the existence of "special needs" has never been found to permit warrantless wiretapping. "Special needs" generally excuse the warrant and individualized suspicion requirements only where those requirements are impracticable and the intrusion on privacy is minimal. *See, e.g., Griffin v. Wisconsin,* 483 U.S. 868, 873 (1987). Wiretapping is not a minimal intrusion on privacy, and the experience of FISA shows that foreign intelligence surveillance can be carried out through warrants based on individualized suspicion.

The court in *Sealed Case* upheld FISA itself, which requires warrants issued by Article III federal judges upon an individualized showing of probable cause that the subject is an "agent of a foreign power." The NSA domestic spying program, by contrast, includes none of these safeguards. It does not require individualized judicial approval, and it does not require a showing that the target is an "agent of a foreign power." According to Attorney General Gonzales, the NSA may wiretap any person in the United States who so much as receives a communication from anyone abroad, if the administration deems either of the parties to be affiliated with al Qaeda, a member of an organization affiliated with al Qaeda, "working in support of al Qaeda," or "part of" an organization or group "that is supportive of al Qaeda."[12] Under this reasoning, a U.S. citizen living here who received a phone call from another U.S. citizen who attends a mosque that the administration believes is "supportive" of al Qaeda could be wiretapped without a warrant. The absence of meaningful safeguards on the NSA program at a minimum raises serious questions about the validity of the program under the Fourth Amendment, and therefore supports an interpretation of the AUMF that does not undercut FISA's regulation of such conduct.

*   *   *

In conclusion, the DOJ letter fails to offer a plausible legal defense of the NSA domestic spying program. If the Administration felt that FISA was insufficient, the proper course was to seek legislative amendment, as it did with other aspects of FISA in the Patriot Act, and as Congress expressly contemplated when it enacted the wartime wiretap provision in FISA. One of the crucial features of a constitutional democracy is that it is always open to the President—or anyone else—to seek to change the law. But it is also beyond dispute that, in such a democracy, the President cannot simply violate criminal laws behind closed doors because he deems them obsolete or impracticable.[13]

---

[12] *See* Gonzales/Hayden Press Briefing, *supra* note 4.

[13] During consideration of FISA, the House of Representatives noted that "the decision as to the standards governing when and how foreign intelligence electronic surveillance should be conducted is and should be a political decision, in the best sense of the term, because it involves the weighing of important public policy concerns–civil liberties and national security. Such a political decision is one properly made by the political branches of Government together, not adopted by one branch on its own and with no regard for the other. Under our Constitution legislation is the embodiment of just such political decisions." H. Rep. 95-1283, pt. I, at 21-22. Attorney General Griffin Bell supported FISA in part because "no matter how well intentioned or ingenious the persons in the Executive branch who formulate these measures, the crucible of the legislative process will ensure that the procedures will be affirmed

        We hope you find these views helpful to your consideration of the legality of the
NSA domestic spying program.

Sincerely,

Curtis A. Bradley
Richard and Marcy Horvitz Professor of Law, Duke University*
Former Counselor on International Law in the State Department Legal Adviser's Office,
2004

David Cole
Professor of Law, Georgetown University Law Center

Walter Dellinger
Douglas Blount Maggs Professor of Law, Duke University
Former Assistant Attorney General, Office of Legal Counsel, 1993-1996
Former Acting Solicitor General of the United States, 1996-97

Ronald Dworkin
Frank Henry Sommer Professor, New York University Law School

Richard Epstein
James Parker Hall Distinguished Service Professor, University of Chicago Law School
Peter and Kirsten Bedford Senior Fellow, Hoover Institution

Harold Hongju Koh
Dean and Gerard C. & Bernice Latrobe Smith Professor of Intl. Law, Yale Law School
Former Assistant Secretary of State for Democracy, Human Rights and Labor 1998-2001
Former Attorney-Adviser, Office of Legal Counsel, DOJ, 1983-85

Philip B. Heymann
James Barr Ames Professor, Harvard Law School
Former Deputy Attorney General, 1993-94

Martin S. Lederman
Visiting Professor, Georgetown University Law Center
Former Attorney Advisor, Department of Justice Office of Legal Counsel, 1994-2002

Beth Nolan
Former Counsel to the President, 1999-2001; Deputy Assistant Attorney General, Office of
Legal Counsel, 1996-1999; Associate Counsel to the President, 1993-1995; Attorney
Advisor, Office of Legal Counsel, 1981-1985

---

by that branch of government which is more directly responsible to the electorate." Foreign Intelligence Surveillance
Act of 1978: Hearings Before the Subcomm. on Intelligence and the Rights of Americans of the Senate Select
Comm. On Intelligence, 95th Cong., 2d Sess. 12 (1977).

William S. Sessions
Former Director, FBI
Former Chief United States District Judge, Western District of Texas

Geoffrey R. Stone
Harry Kalven, Jr. Distinguished Service Professor of Law, University of Chicago
Former Dean of the University of Chicago Law School and Provost of the University of Chicago

Kathleen M. Sullivan
Stanley Morrison Professor, Stanford Law School
Former Dean, Stanford Law School

Laurence H. Tribe
Carl M. Loeb University Professor and Professor of Constitutional Law
Harvard Law School

William W. Van Alstyne
Lee Professor, William and Mary Law School
Former Attorney, Department of Justice, 1958

* Affiliations are noted for identification purposes only.

Cc: Judge Colleen Kollar-Kotelly
        Chief Judge, Foreign Intelligence Surveillance Court
        U.S. Courthouse
        333 Constitution Ave., NW
        Washington, DC 20001